SPORTS INNOVATION MANAGEMENT

This book introduces readers to emerging issues of sport innovation. The book focuses on the role of innovation in the sports context and how we can leverage opportunities that arise from networks and optimize resources by identifying where they are most effective. It helps to identify the conditions and procedures that emergent business ventures need to be formed.

The book is a useful reference for sports organizations, athletes and government organizations promoting the use of innovation to generate competitive advantage in the global marketplace.

Vanessa Ratten is Associate Professor of Entrepreneurship and Innovation at the Department of Management and Marketing, La Trobe Business School, Australia.

SPORTS INNOVATION MANAGEMENT

Vanessa Ratten

LONDON AND NEW YORK

First published 2018
by Routledge
2 Park Square, Milton Park, Abingdon, Oxon OX14 4RN

and by Routledge
711 Third Avenue, New York, NY 10017

Routledge is an imprint of the Taylor & Francis Group, an informa business

© 2018 Vanessa Ratten

The right of Vanessa Ratten to be identified as author of this work has been asserted by her in accordance with sections 77 and 78 of the Copyright, Designs and Patents Act 1988.

All rights reserved. No part of this book may be reprinted or reproduced or utilised in any form or by any electronic, mechanical, or other means, now known or hereafter invented, including photocopying and recording, or in any information storage or retrieval system, without permission in writing from the publishers.

Trademark notice: Product or corporate names may be trademarks or registered trademarks, and are used only for identification and explanation without intent to infringe.

British Library Cataloguing-in-Publication Data
A catalogue record for this book is available from the British Library

Library of Congress Cataloging-in-Publication Data
A catalog record for this book has been requested

ISBN: 978-1-138-03731-1 (hbk)
ISBN: 978-1-138-03732-8 (pbk)
ISBN: 978-1-315-17797-7 (ebk)

Typeset in Bembo
by codeMantra

CONTENTS

List of tables	*vi*
Acknowledgements	*vii*
Foreword	*viii*

1	Sports innovation management: an overview	1
2	Creativity and innovation	15
3	Transformational leadership	30
4	Innovative marketing	44
5	Culture, social and sustainable innovation	58
6	Open innovation	69
7	Corporate entrepreneurship	80
8	Technology innovation	97
9	Future directions for sports innovation management	119

Index *125*

TABLES

2.1	Creativity in sport	21
2.2	Personality traits for sports innovation	23
3.1	Dimensions of sport innovation organizational climates	36
3.2	Attributes of a sports start-up community	40
5.1	Measurement areas of innovation management	64
7.1	Stages of sport-based corporate entrepreneurship	91
8.1	Action and reaction in sports technology innovation	98
8.2	Sport culture	112
8.3	Information technology innovations in sport	114
9.1	Future directions of sport innovation research	121

ACKNOWLEDGEMENTS

I thank Yongling Lam and Samantha Phua for all their help in the writing and editing of this book. I thank my family including my mum, Kaye for always believing in me, my Dad, David for his sport knowledge and my brothers, Stuart and Hamish for telling me to write this book.

FOREWORD

Sports and innovation are two concepts that are deeply rooted in many aspects of our lives, both as individuals and as a society at large. Relative to some other modern concepts, such as strategy, business models, leadership, marketing and sustainability, they go even more explicitly back to how we have developed as human beings and as a society. Innovation, broadly defined, is arguably at the basis of anything we consider normal today. But, of course, at some point in time, people actually invented technologies as the wheel or the light bulb as well as more institutional notions as governments and universities—all commonplace concepts these days.

At the same time, sports have played an important role in shaping important parts of our society, going back to at least the ancient times of Sumer, China, Egypt and Greece. And, currently, sports play an important role in how people spend their free time—the word sport in fact is derived from the Old French desporter, which roughly translates into leisure time—and as such it touches many parts of our lives. So, while sports and innovation have several similarities, they are also very connected, both conceptually and practically. This is not the case through all innovations that have shaped the sports as we currently know them. Again, like anything we currently use, all artifacts used in sports (and even the sports themselves) needed to be invented and implemented at some point in time. This applies to various aspects of sports, including physical attributes, rules, organization, and so on. Involved in all of these aspects is some sort of implicit or explicit management, which is crucial in whether innovations in sports will be a success or a failure—highlighting why a book on Sports Innovation Management makes so much sense.

Sports Innovation Management in a more narrow sense is about how innovations in sports can be managed in a way that improves performance, which may be considered at different levels and from different perspectives. This is important because the sports industry is traditionally one in which innovation can be hard to achieve. There may be several explanations, such as that the cost of failure is high, that there is a strong Not Invented Here syndrome, or that rules and regulations inhibit experimentation and creative behavior. At the same time, sports can be extremely competitive with short performance and evaluation cycles—a context in which innovation could make the difference between being the winner or the loser.

What I personally also like about sports is that it often embeds an entrepreneurial spirit on different levels. As such, I find it very inspirational to discuss (the management of) sports innovation with people who are the innovators and entrepreneurs in this domain. Let me give an example from my home country (which is typically top ranked in some sports) and using my own favorite sport as an example (although we could probably use some innovations to get back to the level where we think we belong). Just the other day, I had a good discussion with Michiel Pieters, who is not only a former academic colleague and current innovation manager but also an entrepreneur—or what one may call a sports entrepreneur—who has tried to make significant impact in the Dutch football club FC Eindhoven of which he is the former chairman. There, he introduced a new way of working at the club with some concrete examples being using data analytics for scouting, using GPS data and social network analysis for physical and tactical analysis and integrating futsal in youth development programs. In this way, he showed that also relatively small clubs (turnover: €3 million in season 2016–2017) are able to make use of most recent innovations within the sports industry. As a practitioner of Sports Innovation Management, he told me that he would consider management development programs as a key topic for the successful management of sports innovation given that many technical directors and (youth) trainers are still unaware of the possibilities of recent technical developments in sports. On the basis of his experience, he moreover emphasized the need to open up innovation management practices at professional sports organizations. Some examples here would be the recently announced innovation hubs at PSV Eindhoven and FC Barcelona, or the group structure at City Football Group that creates knowledge spillovers between different continents and sports.

All in all, with this background and some of these examples, Sports Innovation Management strikes me as a particularly important topic. And while there are certainly good practices to consider, there is great potential for both research and practice to better understand various attributes of sports innovation. Ultimately, it will be the role of management to turn these innovations into improved performance, on various levels such as the individual or team, the club or organization, and the industry or even society at large. In this context, many important questions remain and it is great to see that this book on Sports Innovation Management starts to answer a few of them.

Marcel Bogers
Associate Professor of Innovation and Entrepreneurship
University of Copenhagen
Copenhagen, Denmark

1
SPORTS INNOVATION MANAGEMENT
An overview

Introduction

Innovation is changing the way sport is practiced and how people connect with sport. This is largely the result of sport being a growing industry as a result of increased emphasis on leisure and recreation activities. Innovation has been at the heart of sport because of the role competition plays in the game and also the industry. There are a number of stakeholders in sport that impact innovation including athletes, coaches, managers and researchers. Sports innovation involves a new way of doing something that gives a competitive advantage in the sport context. The ability to innovate is a core need in sport as it enables renewal and change by encouraging new sports to develop and the emergence of alternative playing techniques that is core to the survival of some sports.

Few scholars have attempted to examine sports innovation management at multiple levels of analysis including the individual, organization, institutional and macro-environment. This has limited the research existing on sports innovation management as most focus on technological change. As innovation is essential for the progress of sports management as a field of study it is important to identify areas that require both academic and practitioner attention. This is due to there being a complex interaction between sport and innovation as a result of the popularity of sport in society. This has meant the sport industry needs to more effectively identify ways they need to innovate. Innovation is seen as a solution to problems in sport. The reason for this is that innovation is helpful for economic, social and technical reasons and contributes to a better society. Innovation in sport stimulates new ideas that pave the way for increased enjoyment.

The benefits of sports innovation come from the innovators who face risks bringing their ideas to fruition, who often face uncertainties and need to alter their ideas before they are successful. Some sport innovators have a natural affinity for sport due to their personal associations with sport. This increases the likelihood of their sport innovations getting into the marketplace because of their social networks and personal connections. Many innovations in sport occur by chance as athletes develop products that provide better capabilities. This has led to sport innovations being evaluated in different ways depending on the understanding of success for individuals. The success of sports innovation is linked to better sports performance while others may have financial motives.

This chapter seeks to discuss the increasing importance of innovation in sport, which has influenced the competitiveness of sport in the global economy. The role different types of innovation play in sport are discussed that gives way to an analysis about the concept of sports innovation. The main findings suggest that sports innovation is influenced by the co-creation of knowledge by different entities involved in sport. This suggests that a deeper understanding of sports innovation in an academic, policy and practical setting is required to facilitate global growth. This is crucial as innovation is the competitive advantage that gives sport its distinctive global appeal.

This objective of this chapter is to provide the background for the growing role of innovation in sport. The importance of sports innovation management is discussed as a way to fuel athletic and organizational success. The relationships between innovation and sport are examined that paves the way for a theory of sports innovation. Finally, the chapter closes with an elaboration about the current knowledge on sports innovation.

Goals of this book

In this book, I take a step toward addressing the gap between sports management and innovation management for a number of important reasons. First, the process of innovation influences sport in a multitude of ways. This includes the way sport develops to its interaction with society. The magnitude of sports innovation (incremental or radical) will be influenced by the processes that enable it to gain entry into the marketplace. This means there is a need to understand the antecedents of sports innovation in order to evaluate its outcomes. This can be conducted by focusing on the sports innovation content to see its changing nature within society.

Second, managers of sports organizations who are interested in building innovation into their structures need guidance about how to do this. For both sport and related industries having an innovative mindset helps to make an organization innovative. This can enable managers to evaluate the pros and cons of innovation in order to achieve the best possible outcome for their organization. Innovation managers involved with sports-related services can also gain from an understanding of the financial and non-financial resources needed to invest in innovation. While some managers have a natural tendency for innovation others need to learn it.

Third, there is a global trend toward sport as a leisure activity but also in terms of health and wellness. This growth has coincided with the ageing of the population and more people generally spending a greater degree of time on sports-related activities. This means that there is an effort by sports organizations to tap into this market by offering innovative products and services. Therefore, sports innovation can offer a way for organizations to value add to their market in order to gain potential new customers.

Sport

Sport needs to be innovative to cope with the increased usage of leisure facilities and demand from consumers. In the past, sport was considered more formal but now it has moved to be a leisure activity that can also be informal in nature. This is reflected in the increase in the active leisure wear market as people now wear what was previously considered only sports apparel in their everyday lives. In addition, as a result of the ageing of the population there is an increased emphasis on health and wellness. This has led to more slow sports such as yoga and meditation becoming popular and considered mainstream. The introduction of new sports is an innovation as they have changed people's perception and understanding of sport.

The more recreational nature of sport is reflected in people working more flexible hours than in the past. Traditionally, sport was considered a weekend activity conducted after the Monday to Friday work week but the introduction of longer shopping hours and telecommuting has led to people requiring different hours and places to play sport. Fitness centers are more popular and 24-hour gyms are located in many areas. This has led to innovations in gym equipment and hours opened in order to accommodate more consumers.

The literature on sport has been linked to other disciplines including economics, geography, management and sociology but less emphasis has been placed on innovation, which is unusual due to the importance innovation plays in sport. This view is reflected in Ringuet-Riot et al (2014:817) stating "in the sport context, innovations that are solutions to a pre-identified problem or need are critical to developing sport and for maximizing the experiences and performances of individuals and organizations." Moreover, sport has been impacted by the digital revolution as it has caused more usage of technological innovation. Some sports such as kitesurfing have been innovations that appeal to a sense of freedom and independence among people.

Sport has been innovative as it has undergone many different lifecycles when some are fashionable then become lesser-known but later increase in appeal. Examples are cardio aerobics made popular by Jane Fonda, which was superseded by a focus on yoga but has since reemerged in popularity. Other lifecycle sports are Zumba, which combines dance and aerobics as a form of innovation. In addition, the use of digital technology is evident in video games incorporating physical activity as part of the game. This means that a person can kick a ball that then shows online, which has changed the way people play sport. Often the playing or watching of sport is done in both a physical and online format.

There has been more media attention placed on the importance of people having a healthy lifestyle. This has led to a change in peoples eating habits but also more acceptance of sport into everyday lifestyle activity. More fitness classes such aerobics are now conducted outdoors in order to complement people wanting more natural settings for sport activities. At the same time though, some sports have innovated by going indoors, such as trampoline clubs that used to be more outdoors and holiday-based sporting activities. Other sports such as indoor rock climbing have emerged as a way for people with busy lifestyles to practice sport in a more controlled environment. This is in conjunction with sport being considered more as an entertainment activity.

Sport events now often have performers at half time, which combine music and culture with sport. Depending on the country context, the musicians will put on a performance that gives the sporting event an entertainment feel. Other sports teams have tried to stay traditional such as the Pittsburgh Steelers National Football League (NFL) team, which does not have cheerleaders unlike other football teams. The Pittsburgh Steelers, as a result of their name, history and owners, have chosen to focus on the sport and this appeals to their fan base. Other NFL teams such as the Dallas Cowboys have cheerleaders and they have become popular as a result of their themed calendars and related merchandise. The cheerleaders give a sense of fun to the football games but are also orientated to have more of an entertainment vibe at sporting events. This has resulted in the Dallas Cowboy cheerleaders being athletes who are entertainers and an important component of the sport-entertainment domain.

The increased emphasis on fun and creativity in sport has given rise to some traditional sports combining with entertainment elements to appeal to more people. Examples of these sports are celebrity or themed sports events. Marathons have now changed to offer multiple distance targets to appeal to leisure, professional and family running enthusiasts. There are also marathons offering mud and other natural elements to make it more fun for participants. Ultra marathons and themed marathons supporting a specific charity are other examples of sports innovation. Another sport that has innovated in a similar manner is paintball, which incorporates an artistic and creative element to a recreation activity.

Spaaij and Westerbeek (2010:1357) define sport as "activities that require physical exertion and that are structured and standardized according to internationally agreed rules and regulations." This definition of sport is adopted in this book as it enables a contribution to building up innovation levels as it provides a way of experimenting with new products and services in a more relaxed manner.

Sport is an elusive concept but is generally considered as an activity involving two or more people for competitive reasons (Nadeau et al, 2016). This means that sport can include the participation of people in an outdoors setting or through electronic means such as computer games. Many people around the world play sport according to a set of rules. This enables the procedures of sport to be global in nature, transcending cultural and economic barriers. There are also unwritten rules in sport that are codes of conduct and are important parts of the game. This means that people play sport in different ways depending on their strategies. For some, sport is a leisure activity but for others it is a profession.

Sport can include active and inactive participation from the athletes on the field to the referees and spectators outside the field (O'Reilly et al, 2015). This means that people engage in sport in different ways depending on their needs. In addition, there are a variety of benefits from sport including better social cohesion and increased health benefits. Therefore, sport is considered a global language that has helped with cultural understanding.

The constant trial and error nature of sports innovation means that there is a sense of camaraderie between the sport innovators and the users. This is helpful for the creation of sports innovation as it makes a contribution to society. There is strong evidence that sport provides a platform for innovation opportunities and the emergence of new technology. This is based on the large amounts of money fans, clubs and governments are willing to spend to ensure that their athletes and teams win events.

Despite the positive perception of innovation there are some negative consequences of innovation in sport due to the high-pressure environment, which drives competition. This has meant that there is some debate about what is good or bad innovation in the sports context. The strong bonds people have to a sport mean while most are focused on winning there can be a tendency to keep the status quo. This is changing more with the internationalization of sport opening up new markets and business opportunities.

Sport business

Sport business organizations are answerable both to their stakeholders but also the global community (Spaaij and Westerbeek, 2010). Taylor and McGraw (2006:23) state "the sport industry's distinctiveness is exemplified by features of intangibility, heterogeneity and inseparability of production and consumption." This means that the intangibleness refers to sport being a form of entertainment that is enjoyed through experience. This has resulted in players and spectators taking pleasure in sport and engaging in sport because of an emotional attachment. Heterogeneity refers to the many different kinds of sport people can consume from traditional sports such as tennis to newer adventure sports including kitesurfing. In addition, there are various types of sport ranging from individually orientated ones to team sports. This has led to the increased use of technology in sport, which has given rise to more online and computer games related to sport, such as fantasy football where a person chooses their dream members of a team. The inseparability of the consumption and production of sport means that often to play sport requires an allocation of time and energy engaged in an activity.

Sport is based on rules that govern how a game is played. This requires a coordinated approach to adapting to new innovations while maintaining the rules of the game. Innovation is essential for the sports sector as it is used for progressive development. Innovative sports organizations spend time on research to facilitate the entry into new markets and establishing of new ideas. Moreover, the move for innovation in sport is supported by a general trend toward innovation in the global economy. This is reflected in sports organizations trying to support new ideas as a way to improve overall performance.

More sports consumers are focusing on innovation as a result of competition among sports for consumer dollars. The search for innovation in sport consists of anything from new logos or branding to development of playing techniques. The core of innovation in sport is moving away from established practices in order to incorporate new ways of doing things. Innovativeness in sport involves creating new processes that involve an advancement in the way things are currently conducted. This is due to there being a tendency of sports organizations to be innovative but needing to rely on their creative mindset. Therefore, innovation is crucial to the growth of sports organizations as a result of its role in leveraging new ideas.

Sport industry

The sport industry is comprised of the commercial, non-profit and public sectors, which are often interrelated depending on the sports context. Sport teams have provided a sense of community and belonging based on geographical and historical association (Wann and Weaver, 2009). This community connection has enabled partnerships to develop between sport, business and government entities further facilitating social cohesion. By increasing connections in a community, innovations can incorporate a number of different stakeholders. More companies are finding that utilizing innovation in a sports context can influence their success. In order to facilitate sports innovation there should be a connection between business, government and people. This is due to the sports industry being complex and it includes a range of segments from footwear and clothing, facilities and equipment, nutrition to technology devices.

More sports organizations are becoming innovation motivated as a way to develop business savvy revenue streams. This is a result of the competitive global landscape, leading sports organizations to look for the next big thing as a way to increase their competitiveness. In addition, there are more online resources for sport that has made sport dependent on technology innovation. This has resulted in one of the most rapidly growing areas of business being sport business and innovation is part of this growth.

The sport industry is estimated to be one of the top ten industries in the United States and it affects other industries (Zaharia et al, 2016). This has led to more dialogue in the sport industry about how to foster innovative activities. Sport management has become a more business-orientated discipline due to its focus on profit maximization and competitiveness (Zaharia et al, 2016). This change has been a result of the emphasis on business in sport instead of a pure leisure or physical activity. The future of sport business is connected to innovation as a result of its role in encouraging creativity and strategic thinking.

Innovation

Most definitions of innovation refer to it as the carrying out of new combinations. Broadly, innovation can be considered as the process of renewal and renovation as it allows previous ways of thinking to reemerge and new approaches to improve current conditions (Poutanen et al, 2016). Innovation can involve a dynamic and evolutionary process that incorporates creativity (Link and Siegel, 2007). This means that while in the past research has been considered innovation mostly as a linear and simple process, more recently it has been considered as a non-linear and harder process to explain (Ratten and Ferreira, 2017).

Baregheh et al (2009:1324) state "innovation may involve a wide range of different types of change depending on the organizations resources, capabilities, strategies and requirements." There are a range of innovation definitions but most emphasize the degree of newness (Baregheh et al, 2009). This has led to there being a debate about what is new but it generally refers to something that appears to be different to what is existing in the marketplace. The acceptance of a new idea leads to innovation but it requires implementation to make it practical (Ratten, 2017). Innovation can be an attribute in an organization when it generates new thinking.

There is sometimes confusion between the process of invention and innovation but invention involves creativity and innovation is the process that follows (Baregheh et al, 2009). The implementation of an idea is innovation and it involves learning about new processes. The discovery of an idea is an important way competitive interactions can develop that lead to innovation.

Innovation is a knowledge intensive process as it incorporates information that has been learnt to be applied in a practical setting (Pellissier, 2011). Knowledge is at the core of innovation as it enables interactive changes to be made. This is important in sport as innovation enables adaptations to be made to suit current trends in society. Inventions are linked to innovation if used in a different way. This helps to bridge the knowledge learnt from the invention process by combining both external and internal environmental factors.

There are four main phases of innovation (Hisrich, 2014). First, is the idea generation phase that involves coming up with new ways of looking at things in order to bring about a creative change. In sport, this may involve focusing on what is needed to make teams or athletes more effective. Ideas can come from a variety of sources including athletes, sports managers, coaches and fans. Second, is the selection of the most viable idea. This can involve different sport stakeholders talking about the potential benefits of each idea. The ideas then need to be evaluated in terms of a cost/benefit analysis. Third, there is a transformation of the selected idea into reality. This involves focusing on how the innovation will be applied in a practical sense in a sport setting. Fourth, there is commercialization and implementation of the idea into the sports field. This means pricing of the sports innovation and distributing it to people, organizations and public entities that may adopt it.

Innovation adoption process

A difficult task for sports innovations is forecasting the adoption process. If a sports innovation is radically different to what people are currently using then it will be hard to predict how quickly people will adopt it. Sports innovations that connect to users and are easy to adopt will quickly gain market recognition. Organizations can manipulate the adoption process by providing a cheaper price or giving samples to athletes. In addition, the price of the sports innovation and its impact on performance will affect adoption rates. As technology changes quickly the sports innovation will be influenced by the fast-changing nature of the market.

The lifecycle of an adoption usually goes through the stages of early adopters, late adopters, conservatives and laggards. Early adopters of sports innovation see the potential usefulness quickly and are willing to try things earlier than others. Sports organizations try to encourage famous athletes to adopt sport innovations quickly as they can influence fans and others to adopt them. Sports sponsorship agreements may specify that athletes or teams are required to adopt sports innovations as part of their contract.

Late adopters are those that adopt a sports innovation after it has reached market dominance and is accepted as being useful in the market. Typically late adopters also pay less for sports innovations as the innovation has been tested and improved by the market. Conservatives are those that come later to the adoption process and tend to be risk averse. This means that some sports innovations that were considered radical will become more normal once they have gained acceptance from other consumers.

Innovation contexts

The innovation process involves cultural, institutional, social and spatial contexts (Poutanen et al, 2016). The cultural context for sport includes the historical and personal linkage many people feel to certain sports teams or playing fields. This has meant sport innovation has to consider the cultural context to innovate but also respect the historical associations. This is seen in sports teams using new technologies to make better clothing and equipment but keeping the same brand image. This helps people continue their cultural connection to sport but also ensures the use of up-to-date technologies. The cultural context of sport is changing with increased usage of digital technologies that are competing with traditional approaches to sport. The institutional context of sport is an important enabler and non-enabler of sport innovation. Some institutions in sport, particularly in professional sport, spend money on researching and developing new products that are better for athletes. This is seen in the NFL investing time and money on concussion injuries of football players.

The main institutions in sport are the regulatory authorities that govern the code and conduct of sport. These include the National Basketball Association, which was innovative in their use of the "We Care" campaign to promote social responsibility in sport. Other international institutions such as the International Olympic Federation have been innovative in including new sports in the Olympics. Despite the pressure to be innovative by sport institutions, some are non-enablers. This particularly applies to sports such as tennis and golf that have been reluctant to change the way the game is played. Tennis has ball line technology that has altered the way decisions are made and integrated new media technologies into the game. However, the rules of the game are still similar and have not changed much in terms of time and scoring of the game. Despite this reluctance of institutions to revolutionize the way tennis is played, shorter versions of tennis such as Cardio Tennis have become popular.

Golf has also been reluctant to innovate the game despite some players requesting shorter timed games. The Professional Golf Associate (PGA) is an institution and is the organizer of many prestigious golf events. Most of these golf events are run in a week-to-week mode at golf courses around the world. The television coverage at these events was initially innovative but has since been copied by other sports associations. The Golf Channel was also innovative by providing a dedicated television channel only showing golf, which helped to internationalize the playing of golf.

The World Surf League is another sports institution that changed its name from the Association of Surfing Professionals in 2014 due to increased pressure to internationalize. As a result of the growth of adventure and leisure sports like surfing the name change reflects a more international focus. The increased interest in surfing as a professional sport has seen it having more social media fans than the National Hockey League. The World Surf League has also introduced technological innovations such as a free downloadable app launched in 2015 that provides real time surfing information and interaction with viewers.

The social context of sport is essential for innovation. New ways of playing sport are often developed in communities of people interested in the sport. These user innovations mean that individuals have first-hand experience in developing new sports products. As most sports require two or more people there is an underlying element of social interaction in sport. This social part of sport is inherent in both the playing but also watching of sport. As a result of social media there is also an increasing electronic element of social participation in sport. The social component of sport means that often individuals will innovate due to their love of the sport. This can happen by accident or through experimentation rather than the involvement of high amounts of research and development. As sport is considered both a leisure and business activity the way innovation develops may differ compared to other industry contexts.

The spatial context of sport impacts innovation because of the role of location and climate being important to some sports. Adventure sports such as rock climbing, windsurfing and sailing require the right locations in order to participate in the sport. There has been increasing innovation in adventure sports as more individuals have time and money to travel to previously hard-to-reach locations. This has meant some sports such as rock climbing and mountain bike riding have gained new audiences.

User innovations

User innovations are defined as innovations that are developed for personal needs (Von Hippel, 2005). The role of user innovation is crucial in sport due to the internal need of people and firms to innovate because of a specific need. User innovation is different to producer innovation, which are innovations adopted by others without a personal benefit (De Jong, 2016). In some sports innovation, the sense of community is part of the innovation process. De Jong (2016:406) states "individual end consumers also innovate, typically for non-economic reasons: to satisfy their personal needs, for fun, to learn or develop new skills or competences, or to help others fixing particular problems."

User-driven innovations are a key part of the innovation process for sport firms as they enable co-creation to occur. Von Hippel (2017) refers to this as free innovation because consumers do much of the invention and creativity. This helps share the costs of the innovation process as consumers modify products based on individual needs. The rate of consumer innovation in sport is largely unknown and taken for granted by sports teams. This makes it hard to evaluate the sports innovation process to see how athletes, consumers and teams interact to be innovative.

As a result of the increased usage of self-service technology, the role of user innovation is expected to increase in the sports context. This is because people have a personal reason and enjoyment of sport that makes them want to innovate. In addition, the Internet has made communication among sports fans easier so they can share information about innovations. This will change the center of innovation as both innovation by consumers and by commercial organizations work together (Von Hippel, 2017).

In sport, there is a lot of innovation by consumers that is taken for granted and not acknowledged. This is a result of the non-profit role sport often has in society as it is considered a community good rather than a purely private benefit. This has meant sport is seen as a social good or service that is meant to be enjoyed by everyone in society. This is in contrast to other sectors that have a more narrow scope of appeal and require higher costs in order to participate. As a consequence, sports innovation is unique compared to other types of innovation.

Many innovation managers of sport firms utilize user innovation to complement the innovations that are occurring within their organization. As sport innovation often occurs quickly it can take some time before policy makers catch up and implement policies. This is due to the fast-changing nature of sport where experimentation is considered good for the overall benefit of sport.

Free innovation is part of the culture of sport as many people consider sport a leisure activity that they can enjoy in their own time. This is reflected in the intrinsic satisfaction people get from sport. This enjoyment becomes part of the sport innovation process as the fun is in the experimentation rather than the outcome. Von Hippel (2017) refers to this as the pleasure people get from helping others as part of the innovation process.

The philosophy of helping others is part of sport because often other players are athletes and are the only ones with the expertise to help. For example, in surfing it is often the other surfers who will share information about the weather and water conditions that is unknown unless you have knowledge about surfing. This leads to a culture of learning existing in sport that helps with the innovation process. De Jong (2016) proposes this free innovation is conducted during people's unpaid discretionary time so they can choose how they are involved in the innovation process. For sport innovation, this is crucial as there is no set budget or time limit so people can continually experiment until they come up with the best innovation. This has meant many sport innovations have been developed freely by users without any intellectual protection. This has been beneficial to sport as the innovations are free to anyone.

Sports innovation

Sports innovation involves the creation of a process, product or service that leads to increased competitiveness in a sport context. The application of new innovations in the sport industry is crucial as it is orientated toward creativity and enjoyment. More sports organizations have realized that they need to innovate as a way to react to the uncertain environment. In addition, the competition among sports organizations for fans and advertising revenue has meant that they need to be more innovative. In the continuously changing sports industry, organizations that come up with innovations are more likely to succeed. However, the development of sport innovations can be complex due to the need to weigh up the time required and resources needed for the innovation. This has led to more collaboration between sports entities as a way to combine resources and access new knowledge. The dynamic business environment has meant that many sports innovations such as four fin technology on surfboards are spread quickly in the international market. In addition, there are a number of global trends that have impacted the increase in sport innovation.

Sport has innovated by providing less structured ways to conduct leisure activities. This is due to there being continued acknowledgement of the importance of innovation to sport. Innovation in sport is linked to employment and economic growth, which are key issues for business and government around the world. Sports innovation is a way to respond to environmental and technological change while maintaining market share. This is seen in outdoors skateboarding and BMX tracks that offer a sport but also a sense of social interaction. These outdoors sports have increasingly become integrated with technology to provide better useability. Moreover, technological innovations such as GoPro cameras have changed the way people interact with sport and brought a new dimension into the sports experience. This has led to different ways of viewing sport and changing perceptions about how to enjoy sport.

More experimentation with sport has resulted from technological innovations. There are increased linkages now between technology and development of sport performance. This has led to technology enthusiasts seeing sport as a way they can increase their involvement by affecting the way sport is conducted. This is seen in drone technology being used in sports events such as surfing to capture moments that would previously be inaccessible. By recognizing the need for technology instead of fearing it, sport has innovated and increased its presence in the global marketplace.

Innovation has gained immense attention as a result of its theoretical and practical significance and can lead to sport organizations going beyond their expected performance to deliver superior results. Innovation in sports helps to invoke the belief that anything is possible. The field of sport business is dominated by innovative leaders who affect performance. However, leisure activities are subject to similar lifecycle stages as innovation such as development, maturity and decline. Therefore, people wanting new sports experiences are focusing on technology to provide these avenues.

There is more interactivity between athletes and viewers and this is seen with some football players having their own cameras so viewers can see the game from their perspective. In the digital world this is important as technology is changing at a faster rate and sport needs to keep up with these changes. Adapting to technology changes is important for the sport industry as it is one of the most innovative industries and it has understood the role of innovation in competitiveness. The increased wearing of technology gadgets to measure sports performances such as Fitbits has made people connect sport to innovation. In addition, mobile phone apps linking real-time data to sport and the use of data analytics to understand performance have improved management practices. These sport innovations have been conducted not in isolation but with a community of sports enthusiasts who recognize the need for change. Moreover, sports authorities have recognized they need to collaborate with research bodies and firms to create a better sports experience. This had led to sport having a culture of value co-creation.

Many sports innovations are unplanned and happen by accident. This unplanned nature of sport innovations means that organizations exceed customer's expectations. This increases the likelihood that the sport innovation will be successful in the marketplace when it links to customer's needs and wants. Sports innovation involves the introduction of something novel with the intention to be produced in an economic manner. Part of the process of sports innovation is in the conceptualization and development of the idea. This involves creativity but also understanding market changes in the global sports environment. Often sports fans will have more knowledge about the desires for innovation in the sports context based on gaps in the marketplace. However, there may be indirect knowledge that market research at sports organizations can identify in order to be more aware about potential innovations.

The future of sports management: sports innovation

Sports innovation will continue to be the subject of immense research due to its practical nature and significance in the global economy. From the perspective of organizations it represents a way to link sport to a business setting enabling the opportunity to derive future growth. Sports innovation is a competitive tool that when used in the right way can make a substantial difference to organizations, athletes and the community.

The concept of sports innovation has a positive connotation due to the role both sport and innovation plays in society. This is a result of the unique attributes of sport requiring a distinctive approach to understand its application to other disciplines. Sport unlike other industries has a high level of loyalty among consumers that is based on emotional attachments. This loyalty often comes from the social interaction a consumer feels to sport. In addition, sport has changed from being a pure leisure activity to a business model that requires the involvement of managers. Anagnostopoulos et al (2016:2) state "the sport industry is comprised of three distinct but interrelated sectors, that is, public, nonprofit and commercial." Therefore, sports organizations exist in a complex and changing environment that is rife with performance pressures. This means that, in order to compete, sports organizations have both internal and external pressures for increased performance rates.

The dynamic nature of sports innovation provides a way to redesign sport organizations to be more inspiring. Sports organizations can do this by empowering employees to be more innovative by providing a more proactive workplace. As many people work in sports organizations as a result of their passion for sport it might be easier to instill an innovative culture. An effective way to encourage more sports innovation is to introduce positive feedback for suggestions and changes. This would help nurture the environment for sport to be innovative. The inherent team-based atmosphere of many sports makes collaboration a natural way to induce innovation. The team spirit and community role many sports teams have in society encourages a co-creation process to come up with innovations. In addition, the love people have for sport means that they are willing to test innovations if they will lead to good outcomes.

Conclusion

This chapter focused on the growing importance of innovation to sport and its role in global society. Sport is a product of innovation and there is a symbiotic relationship between sport and innovation. Sports innovation is a result of knowledge, cooperation and co-creation among amateur, professional and government sports organizations. In addition, sports fans and athletes contribute to the development of sports innovation. The remaining chapters of this book will further discuss the different elements of sports innovation.

References

Anagnostopoulos, C., Winand, M. and Papadimitriou, D. (2016) 'Passion in the workplace: Empirical insights from team sport organisations', *European Sport Management Quarterly*, 16(4): 385–412.

Baregheh, A., Rowley, J. and Sambrook, S. (2009) 'Towards a multidisciplinary definition of innovation', *Management Decision*, 47(8): 1323–1339.

De Jong, J.P.J. (2016) 'Surveying innovation in samples of individual and consumers', *European Journal of Innovation Management*, 19(3): 406–423.

Hisrich, R.D. (2014) *Advanced Introduction to Entrepreneurship*, Edward Elgar, Cheltenham.

Link, A. and Siegel, D. (2007) *Innovation, Entrepreneurship and Technological Change*, Oxford University Press, Oxford.

Nadeau, J., O'Reilly, N. and Scott, A. (2016) 'Community sport and the newcomer experience in small cities', *Sport, Business and Management: An International Journal*, 6(2): 110–136.

O'Reilly, N., Berger, I.E., Hernandez, T., Parent, M. and Seguin, B. (2015) 'Urban sportscapes: An environmental deterministic perspective on the management of youth sport participation', *Sport Management Review*, 18(2): 291–307.

Pellissier, R. (2011) 'The implementation of resilience engineering to enhance organizational innovation in a complex environment', *International Journal of Business and Management*, 6(1): 145–164.

Poutanen, P., Soliman, W. and Stahle, P. (2016) 'The complexity of innovation: An assessment and review of the complexity perspective', *European Journal of Innovation Management*, 19(2): 189–213.

Ratten, V. (2017) 'Mobile cloud computing: Innovation and creativity perspectives', *International Journal of Technology Marketing*, 12(1): 60–70.

Ratten, V. and Ferreira, J. (2017) 'Future research directions for innovation and entrepreneurial networks', *International Journal of Business and Globalisation*, 18(1): 1–8.

Ringuet-Riot, C., Cuskelly, G., Auld, C. and Zakus, D. H. (2014) 'Volunteer roles, involvement and commitment in voluntary sport organizations: Evidence of core and peripheral volunteers', *Sport in Society*, 17(1), 116–133.

Spaaij, R. and Westerbeek, H. (2010) 'Sport business and social capital: A contradiction in terms?', *Sport in Society*, 13(9): 1356–1373.

Taylor, T. and McGraw, P. (2006) 'Exploring human resource management practices in nonprofit sport organisations', *Sport Management Review*, 9(3): 229–251.

Von Hippel, E. (2005) 'Deemocratizing innovation: The evolving phenomenon of user innovation', *Journal fur Betriebswirtschaft*, 55(1): 63–78.

Von Hippel, E. (2017) 'Free innovation by consumers—how producers can benefit: Consumers' free innovations represent a potentially valuable resource for industrial innovators', *Research Technology Management*, 60(1): 39–42.

Wann, D.L. and Weaver, S. (2009) 'Understanding the relationship between sport team identification and dimensions of social well-being', *North American Journal of Psychology*, 11(2): 219–230.

Zaharia, N., Kaburakis, A. and Pierce, D. (2016) 'Sport management programs in business schools: Trends and key issues', *Sport Management Education Journal*, 10: 13–28.

2
CREATIVITY AND INNOVATION

Introduction

Sport organizations need to foster conditions that encourage creativity as it leads to innovation. Creativity enables useful ideas related to sport to be developed that help build an innovative capacity for an organization (Ferreira et al, 2017a). Novel ideas are important to sport as there is competitiveness between organizations and within sport to have a winning mentality. This chapter focuses on the role of creativity in sport as it is an important component of innovation.

Creativity involves the ability to identify and develop new concepts, ideas or processes in a novel way (Hisrich, 2014). To be creative there needs to be a degree of novelty that differs from conventional thinking. This might involve identifying new concepts that are useful in the sports context. Some people are more curious than others and this helps influence the creative process. Sports organizations need to be creative in order to distinguish themselves from competitors and can do this by committing to creativity by being more open and engaging about possibilities (Anagnostopoulos et al, 2016).

Originality is part of the creative process as it is an important way sports organizations can authenticate their commitment to innovation. By adopting creative techniques sports organizations have the ability to increase their innovativeness. This motivation for creativity is often influenced by the identification of new trends in the marketplace (Ferreira et al, 2016). This is important to sport because it is an industry constantly changing and evolving based on these trends, which make innovation a competitive necessity.

Creativity can involve improving current processes in sport in order to be more effective. This might involve environmentally friendly components such as recyclable water at sports events or the use of new plays in a football game. The degree of creativity involved will depend on whether there are complex or incremental levels of adjustments to be made (Ferreira et al, 2017b). In sport, as the natural environment plays a key role, being creative can mean changing the way things are done in order to utilize new technology features (Ratten, 2015).

In a sport context, there is the combination of professional and amateur sports clubs that enable an entrepreneurial ecosystem focused on creativity to develop. This helps drive the commitment to creativity as there are various professional and associated bodies interested in facilitating increases in performance. In addition, the passionate nature of sports fans and players mean that they are always in the process of trying out new things as a way to progress their sport (Ratten, 2016). This helps build a community of sports enthusiasts that persevere in the creativity process.

In sport often the creativity is in the form of linking previously unrelated processes together. This is evident in sports such as kitesurfing that have combined windsurfing with kite technology to produce a new sport. The creativity can also involve making people aware of a sport concept that was previously unknown. This might be in the form of sports such as beach volleyball becoming legitimate Olympic sports. Therefore, the ideas and process of creativity will depend on the sports context.

Some sports, due to the nature of being adventure sports, are constantly being creative in the use of new materials and technology. Other sports such as football will still be creative but they will do this by producing different and subtler changes to their sport. This might be creativity in the use of new fabrics in sports apparel that are based on the knowledge that players can find more lightweight and quick drying material useful. The creativity process can involve intuition based on what people feel might work in a sports context. This can be a result of sports players feeling that a new product or training apparatus will improve their game performance. However, some sports innovations, while good ideas, can take a long time to develop, which requires determination to see the results lead to fruition.

Some sports that are played in a more leisure ad-hoc manner such as surfing have specific scores for creative moves on the waves, which add a different dimension to the sport. This is evident in the increase of lifestyle sports such as surfing and yoga focusing on the mind-body connection. In addition, the inquisitiveness of people interested in sport but particularly lifestyle sports has led to new clothing and sports being developed. Different forms of yoga have been created as a way to be innovative and this has resulted in organizations such as Lululemon building their reputation on their yoga pants.

Some new sports such as Ultimate Fighting Championship have been a form of breakthrough sports innovation as they have changed the conceptualization of mixed martial arts and wrestling as a sport. In addition, the introduction of innovations such as the Octagon, which is the boxing ring in the Ultimate Fighting Championships, have pioneered a new sports playing experience. This has also been in conjunction with more female Ultimate Fighting Championship players such as Ronda Rousey becoming global celebrities. Therefore, the creative process in sport can provide valuable results when utilized for radical or breakthrough innovations.

The other less subtle form of innovation that requires creativity is incremental innovations (Ratten et al, 2016). These often occur as the nature of sport means that people are always seeking to increase their performance. Some incremental innovations have involved the use of technology devices in sport such as more high-tech activities to evaluate heartbeat and distance. Other incremental innovations have meant the expansion of product lines such as the NFL selling female clothing as a way to capture more market share.

The sport industry contributes significantly to the global economy and is often considered as more important than the automobile manufacturing and petroleum industries (Berrett et al, 1993). The exact economic contribution of the sport industry is hard to measure as it incorporates both profit and non-profit organizations and influences other industry segments in varying degrees (Baker et al, 2016). In addition, sport is both a product and service so there are various types of organizations involved in this industry (Suchel and Stebbins, 2015). There is extraordinary creativity and innovation potential in sport due to its complex and dynamic nature in the economy. The study of creativity in the process of innovation in the sport industry is a fruitful area of inquiry and is further discussed in this chapter.

Types of sports innovation

The definition of sports innovation needs to emphasize the change and creativity aspects while meeting different types of entities involved in sport including profit, non-profit and government. By integrating multiple components of sport it helps to unify sports innovation as a theory to understand change and creativity in sport. The definition of sports innovation is generally regarded as an innovation related to sport that implements a new or improved product, service, technology or process. Therefore, the results of a sport innovation lead to an improvement in business practices and relationships.

There are six main types of firm-level innovations: product, process, marketing, organizational, institutional and ecological (Monroe-White and Lecy, 2016). Product innovation involves the introduction of a tangible good that has new or improved characteristics. Sport product innovations involve new components from which equipment is made such as lightweight tennis racquets or aluminum baseball bats. These sports product innovations help improve user friendliness by incorporating new materials or technologies into products. New sports equipment such as balls can also be improved with product innovations to enable them to improve performance. Many recent sport product innovations including sailboats have incorporated technology that has enabled more efficient and environmentally friendly usages.

Process innovation refers to the implementation of new or improved delivery methods (Baregheh et al, 2009). Sport process innovations, particularly those involving mobile commerce, have revolutionized the business (Cassiman and Valentini, 2016). This is seen in online tickets and betting for sports that have opened up more interactive markets. In addition, improved process innovations in the form of websites and social media have changed the way fans gain access to information about their clubs. Sports analytics has also been a major process innovation that has given rise to a new way of evaluating performance data for athletes and teams. Fantasy football and online games have been developed that created a new online community. In addition, the increased availability of sports broadcasts to global audiences has increased market audiences for sport business. This is seen with ESPN showing college football and basketball to international audiences thereby increasing the market reach.

Marketing innovations are referred to as new or changes in promotional or advertising messages. Sport has had a lot of creative and innovative marketing campaigns. A good example is the Super Bowl commercials that have a reputation for creative advertisements, many of which are made especially for the game and only shown in the Super Bowl breaks. Other marketing innovations are ambush marketing at sports events when groups of people wear clothing with advertising despite the sport having an official sponsorship agreement. Some sports marketing innovations have included the use of athletes in advertising to give a sense of credibility. This has been seen in Michael Jordan's Air Jordan shoes, which have been consistent best-selling products, marketed as Michael Jordan's own personal shoes.

Organizational innovations are changes made in an organization that integrate new ideas (Chesbrough, 2006; Chesbrough, 2012). Examples of organizational innovation are introducing new management structures to focus on international markets or the changing of governance structures to suit international regulations. In sport, particularly in professional sport, there are organizational innovations such as the introduction of rewards that give employees more opportunities to be creative. Rip Curl is a good example of a sports organizational innovation as it made a choice to go into women's clothing and leisure wear. Rip Curl has devoted more resources to the female market as a result of its high growth and profitability. This has been in conjunction with more people becoming interested in women's surfing. In addition, the rise of organizations such as Lululemon into the yoga wear market has made other sports clothing organizations move into this segment.

Other examples of organizational innovations are companies such as REI, which focuses on outdoor clothing and equipment, being owned by community members. REI have introduced some innovative ideas such as the free exchange of products no matter the condition or when it was bought. Organizational innovation is focused on internal processes such as workplace dynamics and it aims to improve work conditions. Other sports organizations such as Under Armour have focused on high-performance apparel but integrated ex-athletes into their innovation strategies as a way to improve the quality of products. The main aim of organizational innovation is to improve productivity and this can be in terms of happiness or a sense of belonging in an organization.

Institutional or policy innovation are changes that bring about new norms or standards. Examples might include the use of goal-scoring technology introduced as a policy to ensure that correct decisions are made in a sport game. Other sport policy innovations might be to televise sports events at different hours in order to accommodate multiple time zones. Another policy are the gender equity rules in college sports aimed at giving equal funding to male and female sports. Policy innovations might be hard to implement as there can be entrenched practices that have become standard. Therefore, policy innovations in sport are usually slower in being introduced than other types of innovation. The major policy innovations have been in terms of equity in sport including inclusive policies aimed at diversity.

Creativity and sport

To be creative in sport there needs to be a desire to grow a sport through adding new product lines or changing people's perceptions. This has led to some sports having more creativity as a result of the open mindedness of the people involved. Creativity can occur through conformity with standard practices in other industries that are introduced into a sports context. This can involve using plastic technology in the production of boats or the incorporation of lightweight material into sports shoes. The standardization of innovations particularly in terms of technology into other industries ensures that there is a connection between work and home. An example is sports apps on mobile phones that people use to watch sports events live and get real time data.

There is renegade thinking that can also be utilized in a sports context. This kind of divergent approach to sports might involve doing something out of the ordinary. The increase in ultra-sports events such as ultra marathons have pushed endurance events to their full potential. In the past, ironman events, in which swimming, biking and running were all included, were popular but this has changed to focus on ultra events incorporating sports courses that were previously considered unachievable in terms of time and length. In addition, the introduction of reality television and sports-only television channels pioneered by ESPN have altered the connection people have to sports.

Sports leaders, due to their motivational style of leadership, can promote creativity within an organization. Sport leaders who inspire others can include current and past athletes who are recognized as experts in their field. The immense popularity of many athletes means they are natural leaders who can shape future trends. Sport leaders have the ability to produce creative outcomes. Amabile (1988) refers to creativity as the ability to create new and constructive ideas to problems. These new thoughts encourage the promotion of innovation as it is important for organizations to have a creative work environment as it leads to better outcomes. In order to induce a creative work environment there needs to be leadership who can balance ideas with results (Vera and Crossan, 2004).

Hisrich (2014) suggests that there are five major steps in the creative process that lead to innovation. First, there is fact finding, which involves focusing on what the current issues and problems are. In sport, this might include looking at participation and attendance numbers to see if they are increasing or decreasing. After this analysis is done then sports organizations can devise ways to be more creative in order to increase participation rates. It might involve the introduction of specialty days devoted to certain themes at sports events, such as ladies day at horseracing events or free entry to sports fields.

Second, there is problem finding which includes focusing on how to find a solution. This is important in sport, especially in resource-constrained sports that require innovative uses of their scant resources. Some sports may face problems from a lack of access to facilities that mean they need to find alternative ventures. Other sports may be deficient in natural resources in the form of wind, sun, snow or water and require artificial means of production. Third, idea finding involves accessing possible solutions by analyzing their strengths and weaknesses. This means finding ways of playing sport that may have not been considered in the past. For example, indoor volleyball or indoor wave pools provide venues in any weather conditions. Fourth, solution finding means coming up with the best way to solve a problem. This can involve experimenting with ideas such as wind to find the best possible solution. Some sports, such as tennis, have introduced retractable roofs or venues in case of wet weather. Other sports such as Formula One car racing have timed their events to enable more people who live in Asia to watch them in daylight hours. Fifth, acceptance finding means educating people about the solution. Some sports that are new, such as kickball, have had demonstration games played as a way to teach people about the new game. Other sports such as cricket have utilized pink balls instead of the traditional white ball so people can see the balls more clearly. Therefore, the acceptance of a creative idea in sport will depend on how useful people find the innovation.

There has been increased scientific advancement with mobile technology that has affected sport. This has included the use of mobile phones to watch events and discuss the event on social media. Photosharing sites such as Instagram and social networking sites including Twitter have made sport more interactive. These technology innovations have broadened the market appeal for some sports that were previously difficult to watch. In addition, athletes themselves have been creative in their use of social media by directly engaging with fans. This has led to athletes being creative by seeing what appeals to fans but also disseminating knowledge more widely. Creativity involves the use of a person's personality and expertise to come up with ideas. This can depend on environmental factors, such as where a person lives, which impact on the level of creativity.

Creativity requires ideas to be novel but useful, which may be difficult as they are often on opposite ends of the continuum. Some creative sport ideas may be original but costly and hard to produce. In the uncertain business environment it is vital that sport organizations search for ways to be more innovative. Innovative behaviors that introduce new products, services and processes help sport organizations grow and stay competitive. The innovation can include new solutions for business problems that can generate creative ideas.

The dissemination of creativity as a topic in sport is relatively new in the literature despite being used for practical purposes for a long time. Creativity as a business topic is growing in significance as more businesses realize the need for novel thinking and practices. The focus in creativity is on the creative product or service and how it leads to increased performance. Fillis and Rentschler (2005:276) state that in business there are "a small proportion, the entrepreneurially inclined, develop a proactive and skilled approach where innovation and identification of opportunities given them a competitive edge." Therefore, often the actual decisions regarding innovation happen in an ad-hoc and unplanned manner, which are made more complex by the inclusion of creative ideas. This means that many sport innovations are discovered in an opportunistic manner and timing plays an important role.

The terms creativity, innovation and entrepreneurship are sometimes used interchangeably but they are different in meaning (Fillis and Rentschler, 2010). Creativity involves being dynamic in applying new ideas and ways of thinking. As new inventions come into the market it is important for businesses to take a creative approach to introducing them. Knowledge is now the most important resource for organizations, replacing the capital, labor and land (Fillis and Rentschler, 2005). Some people refer to creativity as being a form of art, as it is in the eyes of the beholder whether it is good or bad. This has led to creativity being construed in different ways depending on how it is applied in sport. Some creative clothing in sport, such as high-top sneakers, are now common in the marketplace. This has resulted in creativity being a form of fashion that depends on social conditions. The imagination is a core part of creativity as it enables new ways of looking at things to become marketable products. As many sports organizations become stuck in the same routine creativity provides a way for them to escape the status quo. This can take place when creativity combines with innovation and new thinking to build on established practices (Fillis and Rentschler, 2005). Creativity in sport can involve a person, place, product, process, property or practice and this is summarized in Table 2.1.

TABLE 2.1 Creativity in sport

Type	Examples
Person	Unique or different sports ability, roles or traits
Place	Atmospheric attributes that are different
Product	New tangible sports goods
Process	Innovative steps in making sports products or technologies
Property	Culture promoting new forms of behavior
Practice	Actions and results in sport

Source: Adapted from Fillis and Rentschler (2005).

Proactive personality

Within the sports context it helps to have a proactive personality that can enable innovations to happen more quickly. Tang (2016:56) defines a proactive personality as "the tendency toward taking action to influence ones environment." This is useful in a sports context as often athletes and coaches spend long periods of time interacting with their sports environment, which can lead them to develop innovations. A proactive personality means that an individual will respond to change in a way that has a positive effect. This is helpful for initiating personal success by focusing on how to create a competitive advantage.

Sports managers can use their proactive personalities as a way to build innovations and to ascertain potential future trends. This is helpful as sports managers can scan their environment to see changes in customer demands and playing styles that lead to innovation. There may be some conflict between the development of new sports services as the current services also need to be maintained. This has led to there being a time lag in the conceptualization of a sport innovation and the introduction of it into the marketplace. Some of this time delay has been a result of too much focus on existing sports services through improvement while disregarding new innovations that will supersede the previous ones.

Highly proactive sports organizations focus on existing services by maximizing profitability and also on spending time developing innovations that can reduce costs and improve quality. To do this, proactive managers need to scan the environment for possible opportunities (Tang, 2016). This involves looking for potential gaps in the market and ways to add value. This is important in sport as organizations are constantly competing with each other due to the uncertain business environment. It is also important to focus on social capital building, which involves obtaining both intangible and tangible resources (Tang, 2016). This helps build linkages between what an organization has and what it needs in order to be successful. Proactive managers use established social capital to access information and knowledge that can lead to sport innovations. Social capital can lead to management innovation as it helps to acquire the necessary resources to enable opportunities. Nahapiet and Ghoshal (1998) refer to social capital as the networks that are embedded in relationship structures.

Proactive people guide innovation objectives by advocating for ideas that lead to solutions of problems. This can involve exploring different sports innovation strategies by scanning the global business environment to identify trends. In sport, there may be more ability for people to show initiative due to the high number of people who play in their leisure time and have more flexibility in ability to focus on innovation. Social capital enables the opening up of connections that are needed to realize potential opportunities (Tang, 2016). These network connections enable feasibility studies to be conducted to test out the sport innovation.

Proactive managers utilize social capital as a way to strategically influence the orientation of their organization. This helps to create differentiation in their

TABLE 2.2 Personality traits for sports innovation

Trait	Sport examples
Able to accommodate opposites	Volleyball
Attracted to complexity	Gymnastics
Curiosity	Rock climbing
Energy	Aerobics
Firm sense of self as creative	Waterskiing
High valuation of aesthetic qualities in experience	Surfing
Independence of judgment	Sailing
Intellectual honesty	Chess
Internal locus of control (reflective/introspective)	Tennis
Intuition	Windsurfing
Persistence	Marathon running
Self-confidence	Athletics

Source: Adapted from Ahmed (1998) and Woodman and Schoenfeldt (1990).

organization in order to build high-quality sports innovations. In addition, proactive managers usually have behaviors such as the ability to identify opportunities while maintaining service standards. Social capital includes both internal and external forms, which are utilized in different ways. Internal social capital is the networks and relationships embedded inside an organization (Nahapiet and Ghoshal, 1998). The resources within an organization include the human capital that facilitates ideas sharing and knowledge dissemination. Both social and human capital are found embedded in the personality traits, which lead individuals to prefer certain sports. This is reflected in Table 2.2.

Co-creation

Co-creation is a form of open innovation as it enables firms to communicate with customers about innovation. There has been an increased emphasis on co-creation as it can help build innovation through the engagement between consumers and organizations. This helps consumers to share knowledge with organizations in order to increase business opportunities. Perks, Gruber and Edvardsson (2012:935) link co-creation to innovation by stating it involves "the joint creation of value by the firm and its network of various entities (such as customers, suppliers and distributors) termed actors. Innovations are thus the outcomes of behaviors and interactions between individuals and organizations." User involvement in the co-creation process is important so they can design and test innovations that they have helped to create. Customers can play an active role in the creation process by using their knowledge and experience to provide feedback. The co-creation process can enhance the value of sport innovations.

The process of co-creation involves communication with customers about how to extend and improve current services. Value co-creation is important to go beyond what is currently in the marketplace. Electronic technologies are a way co-creation can develop as customers and organizations work together to provide better online services. Due to the global nature of sport, e-service innovations help build organizations' brand names and reputations in the global marketplace. Many sports clubs such as the New York Giants have a large international fan base and electronic modes of communication are important to these fans. This is helpful to ensure that there are different cultural sports innovations to suit different markets.

Cooperation is part of the process for innovation as it requires groups of people to interact for mutual gain. The benefit from cooperation means that relationships can be developed that might lead to further innovations. The exchanging of knowledge is a way firms can cooperate and share potentially helpful information. Cooperation compatibility involves absorptive capacity, coordination capability and relational capability (Chuang and Lin, 2015). Absorptive capacity refers to the ability of an organization to absorb and utilize knowledge (Zahra and George, 2002). As knowledge is often a strategic weapon for organizations, their absorptive capacity helps them gain market information. This is important given that knowledge is a way organizations can access information in a timely manner that can help them with other innovations. Coordination capability is an organization's ability to manage multiple tasks. As organizations gain information from different sources it is important to ascertain which information is useful. The coordination of multiple stakeholders is part of this capability as each will have different objectives. Relational capability refers to the ability of an organization to manage multiple relationships to produce the best results. Sometimes relationships require mutual trust to develop between partners in order to facilitate information sharing. Organizations that can manage their relationships are able to combine knowledge from different sources (Chuang and Lin, 2015). This helps build networks that organizations can utilize to facilitate knowledge dissemination.

Knowledge sharing

Knowledge sharing involves sharing ideas, which is part of the innovation process. Information that is gathered through an interaction with others helps innovation develop. This communication is linked to innovation but depends on the type and quality of knowledge shared (Mittal and Dhar, 2015). The social interaction of knowledge sharing is important in innovative organizations but needs to be used in the right way in order to affect performance. When knowledge is used in a timely manner it can impact innovation. The exchanging of knowledge enables information to be collected and disseminated to others. This gives rise to novel ideas that are a result of the skills an organization has in collecting knowledge (Bock and Kim, 2002). To be creative there needs to be new knowledge that is jointly created among a group of people. Knowledge sharing shapes sports innovation as people with ideas are involved in a co-creation process. Knowledge is a source of data that can help problem solving in a sporting context.

Innovation is crucial in the technologically orientated competitive environment. The imagination of new products and processes is important to sport as it enables the improvement of organizational behaviors. In sport, there is often a natural tendency to engage in group activity that enables people to work together for innovation reasons. Innovation may emerge from sports enthusiasts solving problems affecting their sport. The attention given to new ideas and the creativity process will influence the level of sport innovation. In addition, the collaborative process in sport innovation means involving people from different areas working together for innovative outcomes. Ideas need to be appropriate in order for them to lead to innovation. This involves focusing on their feasibility and usefulness in sport. Sometimes this can include piggybacking on current ideas.

In the knowledge-based culture that exists in society the creation of knowledge is essential for sports innovation. Knowledge-based assets are created through cooperation and networks in sport among competitors, customers and suppliers. The ability to broaden the sports knowledge base means combining sources of information to support innovation. When sport organizations share information they enhance their knowledge base and bring about relationship-level learning. Therefore, there is a need to manage sports relationships as they are strategic outcomes in the innovation process. The relationship learning strategies of sports organizations play a key role in sport innovation. There are distinctive characteristics of sport innovation versus innovation in general as a result of the emotional and unique attributes of sport. Cooperative strategies enable organizations to co-generate solutions to problems to gain a competitive advantage.

Sports organizations use collaboration as a way to pool knowledge that is helpful in the international marketplace. The two main forms of knowledge are the explicit (know-what) and the tacit (know-how) (Kogut and Zander, 1992). Explicit knowledge is codified and easily transferable making intellectual property protection important for sports organizations. The easily communicated form of explicit knowledge means that it is often found in sports organizations' research and development processes. Tacit knowledge is harder to transfer as it is included in the human and social capital of firms. This means that tacit knowledge is hard to copy and reproduce because it requires inherent knowledge developed from experience and skill. This makes it difficult to imitate as it is uncertain how the knowledge can be replicated. Therefore, the process of applying knowledge will depend if it is in explicit or tacit form. After knowledge has been accrued it can then provide a source of competitive advantage for an organization.

Knowledge can be managed through an exploration or exploitation process. Exploration refers to how to generate knowledge as a way to increase understanding about new concepts. This helps sport organizations discover new activities related to the knowledge. The exploration uses networks and connections to share information and ideas. This enables learning to occur as there is cooperation concerning the knowledge generation. This helps multiple organizations absorb and transfer knowledge. Exploitation means the application of knowledge to create value. This involves using existing knowledge to value add to a sports organization. Knowledge application focuses on individual firm uses of knowledge as a way to increase its information repositories. This enables firms to access different sources of knowledge in order to exploit complementarities.

Explicit knowledge requires little collaboration among firms compared to tacit knowledge, in which collaboration is essential. Tacit knowledge is often embedded in an organization and requires expert advice when accessing it. This is because some forms of tacit knowledge are a complex interplay of multiple types of information.

More sports organizations are focusing on their tacit knowledge, which is a source of their competitiveness. This has derived from the change to intelligent resources such as brand names and goodwill being important to sports organizations. In a sport context, there are different stakeholders involved in the knowledge process, including agents, athletes, club officials, sponsors and team members, and this makes it hard to gain access to all these sources. As a consequence, a sports organization's success will be reliant on the joint accumulation of knowledge from various sources. This has helped sports teams to utilize knowledge for success and the overall welfare of their sport.

Relationship learning activities involve continual joint activities between stakeholders in an organization aimed at sharing information as a way to provide better value. Relationships are important to organizations as they help improve cooperation mechanisms that are important to well-being. Organizations that learn through relationships can develop better ways to increase the flow of quality information among organizations. The capability of organizations in a relationship to learn is dependent on the trust existing among mutual partners. This improves the capability of organizations to manage the learning process in a relationship. Organizations need to maintain and develop their relationships by sharing information that impacts operational efficiency. The way organizations interpret shared information is an important component of relationship learning, and the importance of making sense of shared information to see how it can be used most effectively.

Sports knowledge and innovation

Berrett et al (1993:99) state "it is rare to find an entrepreneur in the sport and leisure industry and particularly the retail sector, who is not active in the area in which they are providing goods or services." Many sport organizations are in the business as a result of their founder's personal interest in sport, which is different to entrepreneurs in other industries. Many entrepreneurs in sport have a passion for it that impacts their personal involvement in business.

Sport organizations need to continue innovating to provide superior products and services in order to sustain their market share. Sports innovations that offer even modest increases are impactful to organizations. However, the quality of the sports innovations is likely to be of a more valuable nature to organizations.

The practical nature of sports innovations has created tremendous opportunities for organizations. More innovations are being developed in a virtual collaboration with computer support. This is due to the increased integration of information and communications technologies into individual lives.

The business literature recognizes the role of innovation as it impacts creative destruction but less is known about the relationship between sport and innovation. Indeed sport innovations are instrumental in business but the mechanisms for understanding them have not received the same amount of attention that other innovations have. This is because the concept of sports innovation is not fully understood by innovation management scholars. Moreover, there is no universal or common definition of sports innovation despite its role in business. The reasons for this lack of focus on sports innovation are unusual as the practice of sport is innovative and impacts performance. Innovation is the key distinguishing feature between a businessperson and an entrepreneur.

The use of sports innovation theory as a lens to study sport is important as it enables an understanding of the environmental context and content. Little is known about the way sport innovation is practiced and defined due to the various types of innovation in sport. This means that more research is required on how being innovative in a sport context may influence positive and negative outcomes. More critical attention with respect to sport innovation is required on how different types of innovation are managed in an organization.

Conclusion

Sport is a popular way people and organizations can be creative. There are many creative ideas utilized in sport but also developed for other industries. This chapter examined how creativity leads to sports innovation through the focus on learning and performance goals. Encouraging creativity in sport leads to the maximization of sports innovation. This is becoming increasingly important as creativity can provide ways for sport organizations to continually focus on innovation as part of their competitive advantage.

References

Ahmed, P.K. (1998) 'Culture and climate for innovation', *European Journal of Innovation Management*, 1(1): 30–43.
Amabile, T.M. (1988) 'A model of creativity and innovation in organizations', *Research in Organisational Behaviour*, 10(1): 123–167.
Anagnostopoulos, C., Winand, M. and Papadimitriou, D. (2016) 'Passion in the workplace: Empirical insights from team sport organizations', *European Sport Management Quarterly*, 16(4): 385–412.
Baker, B.J., McDonald, H. and Funk, D.C. (2016) 'The uniqueness of sport: Testing against marketing's empirical laws', *Sport Management Review*, 19: 378–390.
Baregheh, A., Rowley, J. and Sambrook, S. (2009) 'Towards a multidisciplinary definition of innovation', *Management Decision*, 47(8): 1323–1339.

Berrett, T., Burton, T.L. and Slack, T. (1993) 'Quality products, quality service: Factors leading to entrepreneurial success in the sport and leisure industry', *Leisure Studies*, 12(2): 93–106.

Bock, G.W. and Kim, Y.G. (2002) 'Breaking the myths of rewards: An exploratory study of attitudes about knowledge sharing', *Information Resources Management Journal*, 15(2): 14–21.

Cassiman, B. and Valentini, G. (2016) 'Open innovation: Are inbound and outbound knowledge flows really complementary?', *Strategic Management Journal*, 37: 1034–1046.

Chesbrough, H. (2006) *Open Business Models*, Harvard Business School Press, Boston, MA.

Chesbrough, H. (2012) 'Open innovation: Where we've been and where we're going', *Research Technology Management*, 55(4): 20–27.

Chuang, S.H. and Lin, H. (2015) 'Co-creating e-service innovations: Theory, practice, and impact on firm performance', *International Journal of Information Management*, 35: 277–291.

Ferreira, J., Fernandes, C. and Ratten, V. (2016) 'A co-citation bibliometric analysis of strategic management research', *Scientometrics*, 109(1): 1–32.

Ferreira, J., Fernandes, C. and Ratten, V. (2017a) 'Entrepreneurship, innovation and competitiveness: What is the connection?', *International Journal of Business and Globalisation*, 18(1): 73–95.

Ferreira, J., Ratten, V. and Dana, L-P. (2017b) 'Knowledge spillover based strategic entrepreneurship', *International Entrepreneurship and Management Journal*, 13(1): 161–167.

Fillis, I. and Rentschler, R. (2005) 'Using creativity to achieve an entrepreneurial future for arts marketing', *International Journal of Nonprofit and Voluntary Sector Marketing*, 10(4): 275–287.

Fillis, I. and Rentschler, R. (2010) 'The role of creativity in entrepreneurship', *Journal of Enterprising Culture*, 18(1): 49–81.

Hisrich, R.D. (2014) *Advanced Introduction to Entrepreneurship*, Edward Elgar, Cheltenham.

Kogut, B. and Zander, U. (1992) 'Knowledge of the firm, combinative capabilities, and the replication of technology', *Organization Science*, 3(3): 383–397.

Mittal, S. and Dhar, R.L. (2015) 'Transformational leadership and employee creativity: Mediating role of creative self-efficacy and moderating role of knowledge sharing', *Management Decision*, 53(5): 894–910.

Monroe-White, T. and Lecy, J.D. (2016) 'Social innovation in the zoo', in Young, D.R., Searing, E.A.M. and Brewer, C.V. (Eds.) *The Social Enterprise Zoo: A Guide for Perplexed Scholars, Entrepreneurs, Philanthropists, Leaders, Investors and Policymakers*, pp. 213–235, Edward Elgar, Cheltenham.

Nahapiet, J. and Ghoshal, S. (1998) 'Social capital, intellectual capital, and the organizational advantage', *Academy of Management Review*, 23(2): 242–266.

Perks, H., Gruber, T. and Edvardsson, B. (2012) 'Co-creation in radical service innovation: A systematic analysis of microlevel processes', *Journal of Product Innovation Management*, 29(6): 935–951.

Ratten, V. (2015) 'Athletes as entrepreneurs: The role of social capital and leadership ability', *International Journal of Entrepreneurship and Small Business*, 25(4): 442–455.

Ratten, V. (2016) 'Sport innovation management: Towards a research agenda', *Innovation Policy Management and Practice*, 18(3): 238–250.

Ratten, V., Ferreira, J. and Fernandes, C. (2016) 'Entrepreneurial and network knowledge in emerging economies: A study of the Global Entrepreneurship Monitor', *Review of International Business and Strategy*, 26(3): 392–409.

Suchel, A. and Stebbins, R. (2015) 'The life cycle of leisure activities', *Society and Leisure*, 38(1): 4–6.

Tang, T.W. (2016) 'Making innovation happen through building social capital and scanning environment', *International Journal of Hospitality Management*, 56: 56–65.

Vera, D. and Crossan, M. (2004) 'Strategic leadership and organizational learning', *Academy of Management Review*, 29(2): 222–240.

Woodman, R.W. and Schoenfeldt, L.F. (1990) 'An interactionist model of creative behaviour', *The Journal of Creative Behavior*, 24(1): 10–20.

Zahra, S.A. and George, G. (2002) 'Absorptive capacity: A review, reconceptualization and extension', *Academy of Management Review*, 27(2): 185–203.

3
TRANSFORMATIONAL LEADERSHIP

Introduction

Sports managers aiming to venture into the international market need to be innovative in order to create a competitive advantage. Sometimes the fear of change limits a manager's ability to adopt innovation in the organization. International sports markets tend to be complex and competitive, which means organizations should demonstrate the innovative abilities of their products and services. Innovation allows sports managers to successfully deal with complex markets and offer a superior service to customers. It enables high potential growth to sports organizations that facilitates their growth strategy in the international marketplace.

Innovation in sports is a result of the environment including cognitive, personal and social factors. Cognitive factors focus on how behavior and understanding of one's feelings links to intention to conduct action. This is important as human behavior changes based on adaptive capacities. The way an individual acts or responds helps to determine future behavior. Some people's behavior is also a result of their understanding of a situation in their immediate environment (Gerguri et al, 2017).

Personal factors concern an individual's abilities that influence their propensity to engage in certain actions. These abilities include the knowledge and skills an individual has based on aptitude and experience (Hodge and Ratten, 2015). There is some feedback occurring from these personal attributes as they are impacted by thought processes (Ratten, 2013). Social factors are linked to an individual's cognitive capacity and personal characteristics as they relate to their environment. The social environment includes the cultural, social and physical surroundings, which influence leadership toward sports innovation.

Sports teams are creative when they collectively engage in the development of new ideas. A team environment supports the ideation process as multiple sources of information can be communicated and discussed (Ratten, 2014a). The existence of an inherent team culture helps the discovery of new ideas in sport. This makes it easier to explore novel ideas by collaborating in an environment that is used to team involvement. There are many team sports but also individual athletes refer to their coaching and support staff as their team. This has led to teams being able to exchange thoughts about creative ways to improve the functioning of their sport.

New perspectives about possible sports innovations will lead to more exploratory behaviors about creative discoveries. In order for ideas to be exchanged in a sports team there needs to be a sense of purpose and motivation about the potential innovations. Despite the benefit of having multiple people in teams to exchange ideas there may be negatives to the sports team environment. This is seen in social loafing and relying on others to express their views instead of coming up with individual ideas (Ratten, 2014b). In addition, the sports team environment may hinder idea expression due to high workload and an apprehension about taking on more work. For these reasons, some good ideas may be blocked by sports teams, requiring the idea to be expressed to outside parties who can develop it further.

The desire to keep the status quo and fear of change may be further detrimental to a team environment. The diversity in sport team composition from athletes, trainers and business managers may mean a lack of understanding about some ideas. In order to cultivate the innovation process there needs to be a degree of organization. This could lead to specific people in a team playing a facilitating role in bringing the innovation to fruition. In addition, the relational context of the innovation needs to be managed in order for it to progress. This could be conducted in a careful consideration of different ideas as a way to bring together the most viable option.

Encouraging people to share ideas is important in sport as it can enhance team performance. Sport offers a unique context for team creativity to evolve as there are different types of teams people are involved with, from the team they play for to their team of advisors and the overall team league. This team environment in sport involves coopetition in which people collaborate but also compete. Collaborative behaviors help induce a creative solution for a problem. However, the participative decision-making style of teams may be a hindrance as there can be a halo effect in which all members agree rather than criticize ideas. This means that it is important to place attention on collegiality but also provide leadership for the championing of ideas.

Despite the importance of sports innovation and its increasing attention from researchers, there is little known about the process and the role leadership plays in its development. Some research has focused on sport and innovation but the concepts have not successfully been introduced in a succinct way. This has meant there is a need to address the distinct steps innovation managers could take in order to come up with sports innovation.

Some research has focused on sport business changes, which yields insight into how sport combines a business perspective, but it is challenging to understand the role of sports innovation. From the sports management literature there is an increasing desire to be more interdisciplinary and relevant to business. This has led to more work linking sport management to business disciplines, such as innovation management as a way to understand sports innovation. This new field of sports innovation has positive implications for researchers due to its practical significance in the global economy and provides useful guidance to practitioners.

Leadership is important to bring about sports innovation as it provides direction and guidance. In sport, there are different types of leaders, from team managers, coaches, captains and fan club managers. This diversity in leadership provides a way for sports innovation to be created and managed. This chapter discusses the role of leaders in sport innovation and how they help with motivation, knowledge sharing and integration. The chapter provides an overview of the main leadership styles in sport and how they contribute to innovation.

Sport services

Sport services are sometimes hard to evaluate because the nature of services are intangible and hard to ascertain. Chelladurai and Chang (2005:2) state "sport management is largely concerned with production and exchange of sport services." Chelladurai (1994) suggests that sport services can be divided into participant and spectator types in order to explain them. Participant services include "(a) consumer-pleasure, (b) consumer health-fitness, (c) human skills, (d) human-excellence, (e) human sustenance and (f) human-curative services" (Chelladurai and Chang, 2005:2). Consumer pleasure sport services have become more innovative as there are more integrated media and consumer electronic devices associated with sport. This is seen in consumers wanting more entertainment at games in the form of music and food. Consumer health-fitness sport services involve personal training and gym memberships that provide a way for consumers to maintain fitness goals. There have been innovations such as mobile phone apps that help consumers with their health and fitness objectives. Some fitness apps such as Bikini Body Diet app by Australian fitness instructor Kayla Itsines have become very popular around the world. These innovations have changed the way consumers use health and fitness services.

Human skills are sport services that involve special expertise. They might include people who are experts at doing certain sport-related activities and can demonstrate this to others. Human excellence involves sports services tailored to providing the best in the industry. Human sustenance includes sport services such as access to water and food that are needed in sport. In endurance events there have been innovations including energy bars and mouth gels that have been designed to give quick hydration and nutrition to athletes. Protein powders and other related food supplements have also innovated the sport market. Human-curative services can include physiotherapy and sports massage that are designed to help sports-related injuries. Spectator services relate to sport as entertainment and the associated services consumers require (Chelladurai, 1994). Examples of spectator sports include product licensing and merchandise, plus video games and movies made about sport. In addition, concessions such as season ticket holders' specials and parking are some of the services that consumers require at sports events.

E-service innovation involves process change and service customization (Chuang and Lin, 2015). Process change involves ways of improving services by enabling improvements to online technology. This is important for sports organizations that often rely on websites and social media as a way to connect with fans and market themselves. Service customization involves an organization tailoring services based on customer preferences (Chuang and Lin, 2015). This is important as more sports fans have their own handheld mobile devices and require individualized services. Internet technologies are becoming increasingly innovative in the way they interact with consumers.

Organizations are being pushed to innovate as a result of the digitization of business (Weill and Woerner, 2013). There are more sports consumers who expect a digital experience and online services. This has led to more online sports services that have reshaped the way sport is consumed. More sport is online and this has increased the potential opportunities for organizations to innovate. The blurring of organizational boundaries has enabled sport to become more integrated with other activities. There are now more combinatorial possibilities of how they structure sport. By innovating sports services there is a networked structure of interdependent activities. This enables boundary-spanning exchanges about sport to a broader audience. In addition, there has been the introduction of new ways of viewing sport online that have increased the viewership of sport.

Transformational leadership

Transformational leaders motivate people in their organizations though encouragement and visionary behavior (Vera and Crossan, 2004). This helps employees become motivated to learn by visualizing the future (Mittal and Dhar, 2015). The behavior of transformational leaders has an impact on innovations as it enables creative behavior to flourish. Mittal and Dhar (2015:896) state "transformational leaders are those who can successfully transform the focus of their followers from instant self-interest to an isolated collective vision and inspire them to perform beyond their duties." Effective leaders can influence employees to have more commitment to innovation. They do this by increasing employees' self-confidence and ability to see future goals.

Transformational leadership involves idealized influence, inspirational motivation, intellectual stimulation and individualized consideration (Mittal and

Dhar, 2015). Idealized influence means that a leader is valued and seen as a person of worth in an organization. This charisma means that the leader, through their personality, can make other organizational members do what they tell them to do in a positive manner. By being inspirational the leader enables employees to imagine things they thought were impossible. Intellectual stimulation means to bring in new knowledge as a way to think beyond current conditions. It helps to think in novel ways in order to bring about change. Individualized consideration means focusing on people by name and listening to their concerns. This helps to build trust and loyalty to the leader. Individuals who believe they can produce innovative ideas will more likely succeed. Self-belief is part of this behavior as it enables individuals to be creative in order to facilitate innovation. People with more self-confidence are more likely to follow up with innovative ideas. Transformational leaders who see the value in innovation appreciate independent thinking skills. Some leaders enable employees to spend more time on creative activities as a way to promote innovation (Mittal and Dhar, 2015).

Boies et al (2015) suggest that transformational leadership has four main kinds of interrelated behaviors: idealized influence, inspirational motivations, individualized consideration and intellectual stimulation. Idealized influence refers to a leader acting in a way that encourages others to imitate. Boies et al (2015:2) state "idealized influence is often linked to charisma and focuses on self sacrifice, setting a personal example and leading by example." In sport, idealized influence happens a lot with star athletes in terms of how they behave. Inspirational motivation means the leader inspires and motivates others through having a goal or plan. Often coaches have a vision of where they see an athlete or team going and this enables others to believe and follow them. Individualized consideration involves a leader paying attention to other peoples' needs in a way that inspires them. Individualized consideration is about "personal development and coaching of each team member individually, it may therefore rely more on dyadic relationships" (Boies et al, 2015:2). This individualized treatment in sports coaching roles means there is special attention placed on an athlete in terms of their competences and abilities. Intellectual stimulation involves a leader educating and providing information to their followers. This is important in order to learn about new things that might improve overall sports performance. Some sports teams go overseas and train in new facilities or surroundings as a way to get intellectual stimulation. Alternative methods such as high-altitude training can be used as a way to increase knowledge and open up new possibilities.

The mood of people developing ideas may change based on the stage of the innovation. In the early stages of idea generation there may be a more positive mood but as the idea goes into the next stage it may be harder to sustain this. This is because the sports innovation process requires different levels and types of behaviors. Some behaviors are easier than others in terms of how they influence a sports innovation. This is because sports innovation evolves over time from coming up with the idea and refining it, to bringing it to market. As innovations evolve there are changes in how it is conceptualized. The utilization of individual and team creativity is particularly important for sports innovation as different viewpoints can affect the ideation process. In the initial stage of a sports innovation people are more open to exploring new opportunities. If more attention is placed on the stages of the sports innovation process, a more comprehensive understanding about the different inputs required can be utilized. Sports innovation occurs in a number of different contexts and involves communities that form part of the innovation process. External parties are part of the sports innovation process and must be managed appropriately to control the safeguarding of intellectual property.

Organizational culture

The culture of an organization is an important determinant of whether an innovation will be developed. Deshpande et al (1993) found that some organizational cultures enhance innovativeness better than others. Organizational culture can be divided into four main types: market, adhocracy, clan and hierarchical. Market culture involves sports organizations that are focused on trends and developments in the economy that will impact their performance. Typically, large sports apparel organizations such as Nike and Reebok have been market-orientated as a result of their role in integrating innovation into the development of new products. Adhocracy culture refers to organizations that tend to do the same as others within this industry. This means in sport that there are fewer innovations within these organizations.

Clan culture refers to organizations having similar structures and strategies as other organizations either in the same industry or geographic location. Typically, organizations involved in information and communications technology have acted in a clan way as a result of the need to share resources. This is especially evident in the exchange of knowledge that is needed to make technologically based sport innovations. Hierarchical cultures refer to organizations that are more bureaucratic in nature and typically involve government entities. Some large organizations also operate in a hierarchical way because there is a need to have authority lines for decision making. Table 3.1 outlines the main dimensions of organizational climate that relate to sports innovation.

Sport entrepreneurs who are connected to others in the community and are visible are at the heart of innovation systems. The interconnection between people in an ecosystem enables innovation to develop. Isenberg (2010) suggests that there are nine principles that should be followed when developing an entrepreneurial ecosystem: (1) stop emulating, (2) shape ecosystem, (3) engage with private sector, (4) stress the roots of new ventures, (5) help clusters grow organically, (6) favor high potentials, (7) get a big win on the board, (8) tackle cultural change, (9) reform bureaucratic, legal and regulatory frameworks. The focus on innovation is a key feature of recent academic work on sports management. The sports entrepreneurial ecosystems approach shifts traditional economic thinking about sport to a focus on networks. This is a result of sport being embedded in

TABLE 3.1 Dimensions of sport innovation organizational climates

Dimension	Issues
Hierarchy	Style of decision making (bureaucratic, central, consensus, participative, consultative)
	Individualistic or collectivistic
	Management functions (deterministic, team-based, ad-hoc)
Interpersonal relationships	Communicative open or closed work atmosphere
	Socialization of people within the work environment
	Value and worth of people
Nature of work	Labor or knowledge intensive
	Job roles and flexible work arrangements
	Resource availability of job descriptions
Support and rewards	Performance appraisal
	Actions/behaviors required

Source: Adapted from Ahmed (1998) and Scheider et al (1996).

society and enabled with the institutional and economic environment. Sports innovation is often about new ideas in the making. Stam (2015:1765) defines an entrepreneurial ecosystem as "a set of interdependent actors and factors co-ordinated in such a way that they enable productive entrepreneurship." Sports entrepreneurial activity is the process in which opportunities are created for innovation. Entrepreneurial employees in the sports context are important for new venture creation.

Productive sports innovation relates to any innovation activity that contributes to the output or capacity to build output. Sometimes sports innovation will evolve over a time period in which ideas are trialed and tested. This means that the innovation process involves inspiring new ideas that create subsequent value. In an entrepreneurial ecosystem, there are systemic conditions (networks, leadership, finance, talent, knowledge and support services/intermediaries) that influence entrepreneurial activity (Stam, 2015).

In sport, the networks may develop from current and past players that form a bond over sport. Some of these networks will be affected by coaches or managers who act as leaders in developing innovative ideas. Sports innovation may require additional finance, so it is helpful to have social networks that can facilitate funding sources. Talent is also part of this process and it may involve the ability to follow through on business ideas. For sports innovation to be successful it needs to incorporate knowledge that helps build into a viable business idea. There also needs to be support services/intermediaries that help with knowledge about finance, international markets and regulation, which is useful for turning sports innovations into commercial ventures.

There are also framework conditions (formal institutions, culture, physical infrastructure and demand) that influence the systemic conditions in entrepreneurial ecosystems. Formal institutions include banks and regulatory authorities that govern access to the funding needed to start sport businesses. Culture involves attitudes people have toward entrepreneurship and innovation. In some cultures, people may be risk averse and this limits the number of new businesses, while other cultures might place more emphasis on entrepreneurship and small business. The physical infrastructure in terms of ports, airports and railways also influence the ability of businesses to get products and services to customers. For sport, the physical infrastructure includes playing fields and outdoor facilities. These will differ depending on the type of sport, from golf courses and football fields to the ocean for surfing. Demand for new products and services will also impact the development of systemic conditions leading to entrepreneurial activity.

Innovation strategy involves the resources and decisions around innovation designed in a timely manner. The timed sequence of innovation activities is important in ensuring global competitiveness. Organizations need to make conscious decisions about innovation in order for the strategies to be successful. Adams et al (2006:30) defines innovation strategy as "an organizations innovation posture with regard to its competitive environment in terms of its new product and market development plans." As strategy is subjective, the way an organization manages the innovation will depend on its competitive direction. Organizations need to ensure that decisions about innovation are communicated in a timely manner. Organizations that have an innovation strategy will have differentiation in their goals based on their commitment to change. This may involve an explicit expression about the way innovation is managed in their organization.

Innovation approaches

Johannessen et al (2001) suggest there are four different approaches to innovation: (1) individual-orientated, (2) structure-orientated, (3) interactive-orientated and (4) systems of innovation-orientated. The individual-oriented perspective focuses on the role people play in developing innovations based on their creative capacities. This is evident in sport as often athletes or teams develop sport innovations due to their knowledge and collective learning. Increasingly groups of people are getting together to pool their ideas about sports innovation on public forums such as social media. This has led to more interest in the maker movement as individuals use their ideas for sports business purposes.

The structural perspective discusses the different organizational characteristics conducive to innovation. Some organizations might encourage innovation because of the nature of their business or leadership style. Therefore, some organizations, depending on their structure, will help or hinder innovation (Johannessen et al, 2001). The interactive perspective focuses on how different entities influence innovation. Often for innovation to occur there needs to be knowledge and information shared in order to encourage collective learning.

This has led to interactions in the form of communications being important to innovation. The national and regional innovation systems approach focuses on how geographic areas or policy affects the development of innovation. This is becoming increasingly important with the increase of sporting precincts devoted to leisure activities. More governments and businesses are realizing that sport precincts provide a collaborative way to involve the community, government and business in innovation activities. Johannessen et al (2001:21) state that in national and regional innovation systems "the main focus is on the organization in the environment, interactive learning, knowledge creation, the practical use of knowledge and the distribution of knowledge." This is increasingly important to sport as knowledge provides a competitive advantage in the marketplace.

Innovation is related to change but change does not always result in innovation (Martins and Terblanche, 2003). Martins and Terblanche (2003:67) define innovation as "the implementation of a new and possibly problem-solving idea, practice or material artifact (e.g., a product) which is regarded as new by the relevant unit of adoption and through which change is brought about." Creativity involves some kind of intellectual activity that generates new ideas, which is important in providing insights about how to change or improve something. It is important to utilize new thought processes in sport in order to see how it can evolve.

Innovation interactions

Collaboration is needed for innovation and determines an organization's capacity to be innovative. Sports organizations collaborate with a wide spectrum of others including competitors, government and consumers, which helps to evaluate feasibility of new innovations. Organizations that interact with others in networks tend to be more dynamic and better able to capture innovation. Often an organization's choice of innovation partner will determine their ability to make a successful new product or service.

The geographic position of innovation partners in a network can affect their ability to be innovative. However, research by Moodysson (2008) suggests that geographic location does not always mean innovation. The reason for the change has been more organizations collaborating with international partners through electronic mediums rather than direct physical contact.

Sports practitioners and scholars need to use an innovation lens to understand the dynamic and competitive nature of the industry. Much of the current sport and innovation management research has operated in a silo manner with little interdisciplinary connection between the two fields. The need for an innovation lens in sport is important given the big impact sport has in business and society. Sport influences cultural, economic and political debates as innovation is a way that it evolves. Sport practitioners, scholars and policy makers need to pay more attention to innovation as it controls, regulates and governs sport.

Innovation is an important part of sport since it plays a role in the allocation of resources and strategies of organizations. In addition, the creation of innovation in sport helps to bring about a passionate and motivational workplace that will have longevity. Relatively little work has focused on sport innovation, which is unusual given the role both sport and innovation have in the knowledge economy.

Increased attention to the benefits of sport has boosted the sport industry and created related innovation opportunities. Sport enhances economic development, health, skill development and social cohesion (Campos-Izquierdo et al, 2016). The popular belief of the importance of sport to a community has led to businesses increasing their products and services linked to sport. The importance of innovation in sport is being increasingly recognized by many governments as a way to spur regional development. This is because the sport industry is an area of the economy with small business growth.

There are multiple formal and informal relationships in a sport context that give rise to innovation. Often the learning and innovation that results from these relationships is influenced by collaboration between business, government, universities and society. This is evident in the creation of innovation cycles in which knowledge is spilled over from various relationships (Lundvall, 1992). Knowledge spillovers occur often by accident when different entities work together on projects. These spillovers provide a way to create innovation through economic dynamism.

The knowledge flows between different entities is influenced by the level and quality of interactions (Fritsch and Slavtchev, 2011). Much of the innovation interaction that occurs is within industry clusters as the geographic concentration of organizations, universities and government help to spread knowledge. The geographic concentration of socioeconomic innovation agents has advantages including frequent exchanges of knowledge (Fitjar and Rodriguez-Pose, 2014). This means that the ability of partners as part of the knowledge dissemination process is important for innovation (Fritsch and Slavtchev, 2011). This geographic concentration, when coupled with face-to-face exchanges, is needed for the circulation of knowledge (Fitjar and Rodriguez-Pose, 2014). In addition, the emphasis on geographic clusters of innovation systems has changed as more innovation is becoming complex and linked to the digital economy. This is because information is being transferred through international collaboration. This is important for mutually beneficial cooperative behavior to result that enables information exchange for sports innovation.

Sport start-ups

New businesses or start-ups are an important part of the way transformational leadership can impact sports innovation. Sports start-ups are influenced by the collective learning that is facilitated by leadership in an organization. The key elements of collective learning are cooperation, interaction and networking as they influence the innovativeness of organizations. This helps organizations build their social capital as a result of the knowledge spillovers that encourage collective learning. More organizations are innovating together as a result of the rising risks that make collaboration essential. Collective learning enables organizations to share the goal of generating sports-related innovation that contributes to economic development.

For sports innovation to occur there needs to be an alignment between goals and strategies of the organizations involved. This helps to determine the direction and rate of the sports innovation. Networks are a conduit of knowledge that facilitate sports innovation. This is because the relationships in networks leading to connections with others promote trust and also provide opportunities. One firm by itself cannot possess all the knowledge required for sports innovation and needs to collaborate with other organizations.

Sports innovation depends on the nature of the organizations involved but also on the resources available to the people making the decisions. Start-ups focusing on innovative ideas often need special support due to their lack of resources. This means that sport start-ups, while having networks, need to have the right business connections in order to develop their ideas.

Emerging new technologies are significantly influencing the sport industry and encouraging innovation. These new technologies are proving important to addressing challenges in sport such as environmental concerns and international market access. Organizations can lead the development of sport innovation by collaborating with their vast networks, which can lead to further globalization. Table 3.2 states the main attributes that are important components of sports start-up communities.

TABLE 3.2 Attributes of a sports start-up community

Attribute	Description
Capital	Supportive network of angels, seed investors and venture capitalists
Companies	Small, medium and large organizations in profit and non-profit sectors
Engagement	Meet up, network events, lectures and seminars
Government	Policies to help people start sport businesses including economic development, investment and tax
Intermediaries	Advisors and inventors, incubators, labs, research space
Leadership	People committed to sports ecosystem and business growth
Network density	Engaged group of entrepreneurs, businesses and government officials committed to start up community
Talent	Educated and skilled professionals, training and education, courses available
Support systems	Accounting, consulting and related services to help start ups

Source: Adapted from Stam (2015).

Sports business model innovation

Business model innovation involves new organizational forms or types of organizations for a particular purpose. This can include creating new sports franchises or leagues in order to increase market share. Casadesus-Masanell and Zhu (2013:464) define business model innovation as the "search for new logics of the firm, new ways to create and capture value for its stakeholders and new ways to generate revenues and to define value propositions for customers, suppliers and partners." Business model innovation is a way sports organizations have become creative in tapping into new markets. This is evident in Markides (2006:20) stating "to qualify as an innovation, the new business model must enlarge the existing economic pie, either by attracting new customers into the market or by encouraging existing customers to consumer more."

The changes to business models can be subtle and incremental in nature but have a positive effect on organizations. The key focus of business model innovations is to find ways of delivering value in a way that changes the competitive nature of an industry. Business model innovation can be considered as reconfiguring activities in a business to provide new product or service segments. This is because many organizations view the innovation as being technological due to its influence on efficiency gains. Therefore, for a business model to be innovative, it must be game changing to the industry.

There are both internal and external barriers that limit the ability to conduct sports innovation. Internal barriers include the reliance on existing products rather than investing in radical innovations. This leads some companies to become too dependent on existing products rather than improving their designs to take advantage of market innovations. This is seen in large sport organizations such as Reebok being overtaken by innovative new sports organizations such as Under Armour in some market segments. This means that many sports organizations face the risk of falling into the familiarity trap in which they continue to do things that they are comfortable with rather than taking advantage of technological change. This is evident in sports organizations such as Nike continuing to follow their established business model rather than entering new product categories. Incorporating innovation in sports can be a tricky issue as the right balance between continuing existing business practices and incorporating new ones needs to be made.

The characteristics of the global sports market are changing, and this is influencing its innovative development. This is seen in the design and manufacture of sports products and services that are utilizing emerging technology. Sport can benefit from the cross-fertilization with other industries because it needs to incorporate improved business practices. Moreover, there has been more innovation in sport in line with sustainability initiatives including environmentally friendly events and products. Innovation is also evident in the drive to change the sports market based on comfort and performance. This has led to innovations in sports fashion, which has utilized new technology for clothing and lifestyle purposes. In addition, there is innovation to meet the personalized demands of sport customers, which involves data-driven design principles. This is seen in the increased technification of sport users who want to individualize their sport experience. Hence, there is a need to strengthen the innovation creation process in sport in order to build capacity.

Conclusion

To conclude, this chapter has provided an overview of the role leadership plays in sport innovation. This brings new insight into the linkage between leadership, innovation and sport. The processes of leadership in sport were examined and an analysis impact on different types of innovation was provided. This chapter has helped to establish the importance of human and social capital that is evident in sports leaders who focus on innovation.

References

Adams, R., Bessant, J. and Phelps, R. (2006) 'Innovation management measurement: A review', *International Journal of Management* Reviews, 8(1): 21–47.

Ahmed, P. (1998) 'Culture and climate for innovation', *European Journal of Innovation Management*, 1(1): 30–43.

Boies, K., Fiset, J. and Gill, H. (2015) 'Communication and trust are key: Unlocking the relationship between leadership and team performance and creativity', *The Leadership Quarterly*, 26(6): 1080–1094.

Campos-Izquierdo, A., Gonzalez-Rivera, M. and Taks, M. (2016) 'Multi-functionality and occupations of sport and physical activity professionals in Spain', *European Sport Management Quarterly*, 16(1): 106–126.

Casadesus-Masanell, R. and Zhu, F. (2013) 'Business model innovation and competitive imitation: The case of sponsor-based business models', *Strategic Management Journal*, 34(4): 464–482.

Chelladurai, P. (1994) 'Sport management: Defining the field', *European Journal for Sport Management*, 1: 7–21.

Chelladurai, P. and Chang, K. (2005) 'Targets and standards of quality in sport services', *Sport Management Review*, 3: 1–22.

Chuang, S.H. and Lin, H.N. (2015) 'Co-creating e-service innovations: Theory, practice and impact on firm performance', *International Journal of Information Management*, 35(3): 277–291.

Deshpande, R., Farley, J.U. and Webster, F.E. (1993) 'Corporate culture, customer orientation, and innovativeness in Japanese firms: A quadrad analysis', *The Journal of Marketing*, 57(1): 23–37.

Fitjar, R.D. and Rodriguez-Pose, A. (2014) 'The geographic dimension of innovation collaboration: Networking and innovation in Norway', *Urban Studies*, 51(12): 2572–2595.

Fritsch, M. and Slavtchev, V. (2011) 'Determinants of the efficiency of regional innovation system', *Regional Studies*, 45(7): 905–918.

Gerguri, Rashiti, S., Ramadani, V., Abazi-Alili, H., Dana, L-P. and Ratten, V. (2017) 'ICT, innovation and firm performance: The transition economies context', *Thunderbird International Business Review*, 59(1): 93–102.

Hodge, J. and Ratten, V. (2015) 'Time pressure and improvisation: Enhancing creativity, adaption and innovation at high speed', *Development and Learning in Organisations*, 29(6): 7–9

Isenberg, D.J. (2010) 'How to start an entrepreneurial revolution', *Harvard Business Review*, 88(6): 40–50.

Johannessen, J.A., Olsen, B. and Lumpkin, G.T. (2001) 'Innovation as newness: What is new, how new, and new to whom?', *European Journal of Innovation Management*, 4(1): 20–31.

Lundvall, B.A. (1992) *National Systems of Innovation: An Analytical Framework*, Pinter, London.

Markides, C. (2006) 'Disruptive innovation: In need of better theory', *Journal of Product Innovation Management*, 23(1): 19–25.

Martins, E.C. and Terblanche, F. (2003) 'Building organizational culture that stimulates creativity and innovation', *European Journal of Innovation Management*, 6(1): 64–74.

Mittal, S. and Dhar, R.L. (2015) 'Transformational leadership and employee creativity: Mediating role of creative self-efficacy and moderating role of knowledge sharing', *Management Decision*, 53(5): 894–910.

Moodysson, J. (2008) 'Principles and practices of knowledge creation: On the organization of "buzz" and "pipelines" in life science communities', *Economic Geography*, 84(4): 449–469.

Ratten, V. (2013) 'The development of social e-enterprises, mobile communication and social networks: A social cognitive perspective of technological innovation', *Journal of Electronic Commerce in Organizations*, 11(3): 68–77.

Ratten, V. (2014a) 'Behavioural intentions to adopt technological innovations: The role of trust, innovation and performance', *International Journal of Enterprise Information Systems*, 10(3): 1–12.

Ratten, V. (2014b) 'Encouraging collaborative entrepreneurship in developing countries: The current challenges and a research agenda', *Journal of Entrepreneurship in Emerging Economies*, 6(3): 298–308.

Scheider, B., Brief, A.P. and Guzzo, R.A. (1996) 'Creating a climate and culture for sustainable organizational change', *Organizational Dynamics*, 24(4): 7–19.

Stam, E. (2015) 'Entrepreneurial ecosystems and regional policy: A sympathetic critique', *European Planning Studies*, 23(9): 1759–1769.

Vera, D. and Crossan, M. (2004) 'Strategic leadership and organizational learning', *Academy of Management Review*, 29(2): 222–240.

Weill, P. and Woerner, S.L. (2013) 'Optimizing your digital business model', *MIT Sloan Management Review*, 54(3): 71–78.

4
INNOVATIVE MARKETING

Introduction

Innovation is important for sport as more consumers, businesses and countries are relying on sport for their economic development. Research on sports innovation focuses on the need to constantly innovate but there is also an emphasis on innovative marketing within sport (Ratten, 2016). The intense competition in the sports industry has stimulated organizations to utilize innovative marketing campaigns in order to increase their business performance. Organizational innovation involves new developments in business practices or external relationships that lead to better performance. Some sports organizations have innovated in the way they apportion responsibilities by giving incentives for athlete recruitment or team performance. Other sport organizations have been innovative with athletes through marketing campaigns or enabling them to become part owners in their organization rather than paying them directly for their performance.

There are many different conceptualizations of innovation leading to it having a smorgasbord of meanings (Ratten, 2016). In sports innovation, it is considered a strategic orientation as it involves change. This strategic orientation stems from the intended actions that organizations implement from the design of a sport innovation to its commercialization in the marketplace. Sometimes these actions can be realized when the strategy is determined by management planning. In order for sports innovation to be successful it needs to be created and delivered to the right people at the appropriate time. This means that the strategy of introducing sports innovation into the market needs to deliver the appropriate value. Hence, timing of a sports innovation can be a strategic weapon used by organizations. This has led to there being different interpretations of sports innovation such as innovation by individuals or innovation as a management function. Often sports innovations occur in a personal way as they are developed by athletes themselves to solve a problem. This means that the innovations can develop in an ad-hoc way based on the resources available to the innovator and their integrated marketing campaign (Ratten and Ferreira, 2016).

Sports people including athletes, coaches and managers act as ecosystem connectors. This enables them to connect dispersed sources of knowledge in order to build innovative ideas. In the interconnected world, there is a growing recognition in sport management for the need to understand innovation and the role it plays in society. Research that informs our understanding about the nature of innovation in sport is fundamental and can influence marketing efforts. This is because innovation differs depending on environmental context and this adds a level of complexity to sport.

The phases of sport innovation from conception and design to implementation need to be considered based on environmental context and marketing. Therefore, approaches to the understanding of innovation in different sport settings are required to advance our knowledge about sports innovation. There are challenges and opportunities in sport innovation research as it is a valuable field worthy of study. This is a result of sports innovation being a contemporary approach to understanding the way change and creativity work in sport. Sport innovation researchers can further examine the role of environments in producing sport-specific innovation. This can enable a focus on current approaches to sports innovation and shift the focus to creativity. In addition, this contributes to a better understanding regarding innovation in sport because the traditional boundaries of sport research are being expanded to involve innovation as a reaction to technology, internationalization and change.

This chapter investigates the relationship between different types of innovation, technological change and marketing efforts toward sport. This can assist in understanding the role innovation plays in sport and the impact of marketing, particularly for services and e-service sport innovation. The link between marketing and sports innovation is analyzed in order to aid understanding of the importance of emerging technologies to sport.

Innovativeness

There is a need to innovate in sport in order to ride the uncertain economic circumstances in the global market. Innovation is a way organizations survive but less is understood specifically about sports innovation. Only a small number of sports organizations manage to commercialize their innovations and leverage this capacity for growth. This means that understanding how an organization's sport innovation capability works is helpful. Without innovation in sport the decline of sport is inevitable due to the competition existing in the industry. However, there is a lack of knowledge about the intention to innovate and actual innovation in sports. This chapter bridges this gap by discussing the growth, nature and process of sports innovation in terms of marketing.

There are three major elements of innovation: change, newness and success (Assink, 2006). The dynamic environment in sport makes change inevitable. Innovation is a way for organizations to preempt change and drive future profitability. Customers need to value change in order for it to be integrated into the market. Sports innovation involves the process of creating new behaviors, products or services that are valued in the marketplace. Newness in sport is a feature of the industry as there are new sports being developed that bridge the old and new. There is also the generation of new behavior that puts energy into the sports world. This is seen in new stadiums being built to accommodate environmental and technological innovation. Success is important to sport as teams are valued based on performance, and competition is at the heart of the industry. The first successful application of a new sports practice helps increase viewership and sports participation but marketing its innovativeness is an important component.

Innovativeness is a personality trait as it refers to being innately able to change things based on behavioral characteristics. Consumer innovativeness is defined as "the tendency to buy new products in a particular product category soon after they appear in the market and relatively earlier than most other consumers in the market segment" (Foxall et al, 1998:41). This type of innovativeness is particularly important in sport as a result of the large number of new products and services coming into the marketplace that relate to different sports and are adopted by consumers.

Despite the increased interest, sports innovation is still an emerging theoretical field. Sports innovativeness involves the creation of viable ideas that can potentially be profitable in the long term. Even though sports innovation is of great interest, it has not always been popular due to the focus on other areas of study. The role of sports innovation in society has changed due to the realization that continuous transformation is important. This is a result of the dynamic nature of sport and the role of economic, environmental, institutional, social and technological change. Innovations can help an organization increase their revenues from new products or services but it might take a while for consumers to accept them. In order to evaluate the acceptance of new products it is useful to analyze their usefulness or originality to consumers.

Product usefulness is defined as "the consumers perception that a product or service provides a benefit that fulfills his/her needs" (Li et al, 2015:215). Product usefulness is related to the positive feelings a consumer has toward a product. This affects their adoption decision to use a product based on its specific features. These attitudes help influence a consumer's intention to purchase a product and the complementary uses it has with other products. It is advantageous for consumers to evaluate a product for its usefulness so it can be adopted more quickly.

An example of a sports innovation that has utilized its product usefulness to create a new product market is GoPro. GoPro has changed the action sports market with its portable cameras. They launched their first product, the Hero, in 2004. GoPro founder Nick Woodman is a billionaire and his cameras are used in a variety of sports including snowboarding and yachting. GoPro cameras enable people to record themselves playing sport. It has since expanded its product range to drones and virtual reality. The GoPro Karma is their most recent product innovation—a drone that lets users take aerial videos.

Product originality is defined as the perceived newness or uniqueness relative to previous offerings (Li et al, 2015). Product originality is determined by a person's perception of how new the product is compared to others in the market. This means that original products tend to have more technological innovation than other products as this is the way they can be differentiated in the market. Advanced technology helps a product change or adapt in a way that helps consumers believe it is different.

Nike has conducted product innovation and been original by the 2016 introduction of its 12Soles collection, which incorporates the past, present and future of basketball. This is innovative as it reintroduces shoes that were linked to cultural moments in the history of the company. Products in this range include the Air Jordan IX Retro, Air Max 2 Uptempo and Air Foamposite Pro. This product innovation strategy enables the use of new shoe technology with famous designs.

Process innovations are strategically significant for sport as they incorporate new methods of producing and delivering services. There are two main types of process innovations: technological and organizational (Christofi et al, 2015). Technological process innovations involve new products used in the production process such as software (Christofi et al, 2015). The increase in mobile communications and people having mobile phones with internet capability has resulted in more technological process innovations related to sport. These relate to interactive technology such as mobile phone apps that enable a more efficient viewing experience. Organizational processes involve new ways of organizing a business structure including new production methods (Christofi et al, 2015). The aim of most process innovations in sport is to decrease cost while increasing profitability. There may also be more reliable ways of producing products or communicating to consumers.

An example of process innovation involves the use of sustainability practices in sport. The Sacramento Kings basketball team has been pioneering the use of sustainable innovation practices. This includes leveraging the weather in Sacramento to facilitate better usage. For example, they use advanced lighting controls, low-flow plumbing fixtures and solar panels. The Sacramento Kings pursued Leadership in Energy and Environmental Design (LEED) gold certification, which is one of the highest green building certifications and became the first to receive arena certification for their Golden 1 Credit Union Center. The drive for sustainable innovation for the Sacramento Kings has come from their fans, who want more consideration of the environment in the sports context.

Technological innovation

Assink (2006:216) states "technical innovation does not create value directly; all it does is create change in processes, functionality or utility." Innovations, while helping build a competitive advantage, can also increase uncertainty due to the time and investment spent on development. The market pressure to innovate means that it can be difficult to estimate its potential usefulness in the marketplace. This is especially evident in sport where market acceptance is crucial for the innovations long-term performance. This has led to there being a knowledge gap between sports innovation practice and theory. Many sports organizations have a non-profit or amateur status, which means they are not set up to adapt quickly. This means that while some sports innovations are produced in an amateur context, the trend is for profit-orientated organizations to commercialize the technological innovation.

Technology is defined as "an assemblage of practices and components" (Arthur, 2009:28). Sports technology is becoming more important and integral to the practice of sport. This is because sports technology is fulfilling human purposes, such as goal-line technology or media-based technology. Vargo et al (2015:66) state "the term 'technology' can refer to a wide class of phenomena both 'software' (i.e. processes or methods) and 'hardware' (i.e. physical devices)." Technology provides potentially useful knowledge that helps to solve problems (Vargo et al, 2015). This knowledge means that the way sport progresses is dependent on technological evolution. Despite the intangible nature of knowledge being hard to transfer without proper skills, there are also tangible elements of technology in the physical sports products. The physical elements in technological innovation are ways that knowledge and skills are conveyed (Orlikowski, 1992).

There are different types of technology, from physical, electronic and medical, to social and institutional, and these have different applications in a sports context. Technology is socially constructed based on the way people in society view its development. This results in technology being a medium and outcome in socially embedded practices (Vargo et al, 2015). Sports technology is a form of innovation as it creates value; technology having different meanings depending on its design and use. This is reflected in technology being influenced by institutional structures including beliefs, meanings, norms, social rules and values (Vargo et al, 2015).

The trend toward technological components of sport has meant more emphasis on innovation. This has led to more money being spent on multimedia devices as a way to integrate technology into sport. In addition, consumers have high expectations of innovations in sport as a result of their appetite for increased performance. This has led to it not just being about watching sport but also integrating technology, multimedia and additional services in a sport context. Sports innovation needs to be managed as a multifaceted spectrum of interlinked mediums that incorporates technological advances.

Over the last decade, technological changes have altered sport and one of the most significant of these has been the Internet of Things (IoT) whereby communications technology devices are connected. This has led to people watching or playing sport but using technology for other reasons, such as looking up statistics or viewing the game in a different manner. Increasingly, more sports providers are focusing on innovations related to the internet and other connected devices.

This has increased the potential of new sport revenues from websites and related services.

As there is competition between sports it has become a game in itself to be more innovative. This has reinforced a need for an innovation approach to the management of sport. Apart from internet technology, other technological changes that will have an impact on sport include the use of biometrics and personalized technological devices. This is a result of technology offering a more personal communication and viewing experience based on appeal. For example, people can watch one player and zoom in on this player to see exactly what they are doing rather than being told how to watch a sports event. There is also growing use of technology, rather than relying on humans, to make decisions in games. This is seen in the replaying of parts of games and giving players the right to appeal game decisions.

An example of technological innovation in sport is Facebook, which is adding more live sports games streaming to its services. In 2017, it signed a deal with Univision Communications to broadcast 46 Liga MX games from Mexico's top soccer league. The commentary will be in English and the live streaming is only for US audiences. Live streaming of football has been popular for Facebook and provided an innovative growth opportunity for the social networking website. Normally there is no advertising during the live streaming. Live streaming sport events is popular because of the large audiences it attracts. However, because the broadcast rights for most sports events are under contract, Facebook has to look for alternative entry points. In 2017, Facebook will be showing LaLiga Spanish football events for free. This is a result of the Spanish football league saying they want to innovate by introducing new formats to increase viewership and availability of sports events.

Entrepreneurial marketing

Entrepreneurial marketing involves marketing with an entrepreneurial mindset. Kraus et al (2009:1) define entrepreneurial marketing as "the organizational function of marketing by taking into account innovativeness, risk taking, proactiveness and the pursuit of opportunities without regard for the resources currently controlled." The main types of entrepreneurial marketing in sport are guerilla, buzz, and viral.

Guerilla marketing has the main characteristics of "bootstrapping, creative/ leveraging use of available resources and a highly targeted mix of innovative and effective communication techniques, networking, using energy and imagination" (Kraus et al, 2009:11). Most guerilla marketing in sport is low cost but designed for maximized publicity. The emphasis on high impact in guerilla marketing has seen it being utilized at sports events by people who wear or do things to get attention for specific brands or causes. Kraus et al (2009) mentions a number of guerilla marketing examples in the sports context including the use of henna tattoos on sports people that bypassed advertising contracts, sponsorship of an 80-year-old marathon runner instead of the main sponsorship of the event and a brand on a streaker's body at a football match.

Buzz marketing is "the attempt to stimulate the recipients through the use of spectacular actions so much that the product becomes the subject of discussion or gossip" (Kraus et al, 2009:12). The goal of buzz marketing is to make everyone talk about a product or service in order to build publicity. This creates enthusiasm that can spread through word of mouth. The reason for the increase in the use of buzz marketing in sport is linked with many people not watching traditional media outlets and relying on other forms of communication. This has led to a tendency for consumers to be skeptical of classical advertising and respond to more innovative sport marketing campaigns. The key difference between buzz and classical marketing is that consumers do the advertising and this creates a snowball effect. Increased usage of online and social media has meant that this type of sports marketing has become more popular.

Buzz marketing involves trying to spread rumors about new products or services in order for it to appeal to consumers. Sport products that are perceived as innovative are more likely to be talked about by consumers. This helps to create an air of excitement about the introduction of new sports products into the marketplace. The focus in buzz marketing is on credibility as opinion leaders talk about new sports products. Social media helps with this process as opinion leaders such as high-profile athletes tweet about new products. These opinion leaders have a large number of followers who respect what the person says about the new products. This creates a wave affect as more people tweet or message others about the new innovation. This ripple effect leads to social networks disseminating information about the new sports product into the marketplace. An example of buzz marketing is Betfair's 2015 London marathon marketing campaign, which gave runners a complimentary bet to place on themselves, giving the winnings to charity. Runners entered information about themselves, such as training efforts, in order to generate the betting odds. The focus of the marketing was on customers unleashing their potential by betting on themselves.

Viral marketing is "marketing that uses social networks (family, friends, neighbours, colleagues) to draw attention towards brands, products or campaigns by spreading messages—mostly through word-of-mouth marketing—like a virus" (Kraus et al, 2009:13). Viral marketing involves spreading messages through voluntary communication among a group of people (Kraus et al, 2009). In viral marketing the emphasis is placed on people listening more closely to others in their social networks about new sports products, meaning that information about these innovations will spread more quickly. Social media helps to spread viral marketing campaigns in a cheap and efficient manner. The way a message about a sports innovation is spread will depend on what kind of benefit there is to be obtained. For some sports innovations the message may be uncontrollable and not planned but for others it may be a form of paid advertising.

Brand innovation

Sports brands such as Nike, Reebok and Under Armour are some of the most recognized and valuable brands in the world. Brand value is shaped by the innovativeness of an organization that enables it to adapt and grow. Brand innovativeness is defined as "the extent to which a brand has earned a reputation with consumers for introducing valued new offerings to the market" (Barone and Jewell, 2013:2). In sport, the brand innovativeness usually has an emotional response from consumers who feel a certain way toward the brand. This is a result of the brands' advertising and marketing linking into consumers' lifestyles and attitudes toward a sport. An example is the skateboard brand Vans, which appeals to people who want an urban and edgy appeal.

Brand innovativeness is important in sport as it enhances the image of an organization and its appeal in the market. Other brands such as Under Armour build their reputation on producing innovative products designed for college sport. This means that sport brands that have different marketing or product campaigns are likely to be seen as more innovative. However, established brands such as Nike have been innovative in their use of Lance Armstong's Live Strong campaign, which integrated sport products with a black and yellow color, symbolizing the social cause of fighting cancer. The branding of Nike products with these characteristics enabled customers to see the Nike brand as being more aligned and innovative with social causes. Innovative sports brands have also utilized product placement as a way to market their products in different ways. This is seen in the use of Gatorade being given to football players but thrown over the winning coach in games as a symbolic ritual. Sports brands are using marketing as a result of the increased usage of social media during sports events. This is seen with Sport England launching a campaign to increase women's participation in sport. Their marketing slogan was "I jiggle, therefore I am" and tried to market sport to all females regardless of their body shape rather than just professional athletes.

Marketing innovation

Many marketing innovations are accidental as they have originated from serendipitous encounters rather than being planned activities. This has often meant that marketing innovations come from outside the organizational or industry context and are then altered to suit the current business trends in the marketplace. There are different ways sport can utilize marketing innovation, as it is understood differently depending on the discipline perspective of business, psychology or sociology. Business researchers consider sports innovation from a commercialization viewpoint but psychology and sociology researchers consider it a process. Sports innovation is one of the most important topics in sport and business research. Therefore, the marketing of sports innovation is the cornerstone of continued development in the sport context. This is because innovation plays an important role in sustainable competitive advantage and generating value.

Christofi et al (2015:358) states "by discovering new solutions to problems, innovation can enhance or damage existing markets, transform industries or underpin the emergence of new ones." Sports innovation provides a good basis for the way sports organizations compete.

Innovation is a top priority for many sports organizations. To be innovative, organizations need to be creative and market their products in the appropriate manner. Christofi et al (2015:366) states that marketing innovation includes "the effectuation of new marketing methods involving important changes in packaging, product design, product promotion, product pricing or product placement." There is a significant amount of research and media attention devoted to sport and innovation. However, much of this research treats sport and innovation as separate entities with little overlap. The interdependence of sport on innovation and vice versa means there is a need to integrate both into sports innovation. The purpose of sports marketing innovation is to analyze sports innovation as a new perspective.

Central to the idea of sports innovation is the emergence of a new idea. The process of coming up with ideas in a sports context requires knowledge and guidance. This involves having people with an innovative mindset that integrates sport. Creativity is a precursor of sports innovation as it is the process of coming up with new ideas. Sports innovation involves the production of creative ideas into the marketplace and inherently involves some degree of business. The process of sports innovation needs to have a fast failure approach as new ideas are trialed and tested with resulting feedback. This enables good ideas to be followed up and unrealistic ideas delayed for a later time.

Many of the world's most recognized sports organizations are described as innovators, such as Nike, Reebok and Under Armour. Sports organizations come from a range of sectors including consumer products, manufacturing, relating, services and technology. There is a concern among sport organizations that they need to innovate fast in order to stay competitive. Therefore, it is important for sports organizations to take initiatives to innovate in order to make use of emerging technologies and ideas. The leadership in sports organizations needs to be strategic about how to introduce innovations in order to exploit growth opportunities.

The past decade has seen significant developments in terms of technological advancements, which have affected the sports industry. Many sports organizations emphasize the need to search and discover improvements in their strategy statements. This has led to sports innovation requiring experimentation and risk taking. In order for the sports innovation activities to develop they need to explore thought-provoking ideas. There can be a tension in organizations trying to be innovative as they weigh up the benefits and costs of the innovation.

Creative sport ideas are likely to be easier to implement when they incorporate incremental innovations. This is due to radical innovations having a typically higher failure rate. Patagonia, the outdoors sports company, has innovated wetsuit material by using natural sustainable tree rubber. Other wetsuits use neoprene, which is not an environmentally friendly form of rubber. Patagonia markets their wetsuits in surfing magazines, which is different to their more outdoors and mainstream sports market. The sustainable tree rubber they produce is organic and produced in an environmentally friendly manner.

Organizations need to deal with the uncertainty of the innovation process that takes time to implement. Contextual factors such as innovation complexity and potential profitability affect the timing of the sports innovation into the marketplace. The social context is important as it affects the relationships developed between firms that lead to a sports innovation. Often the results of the creativity process mean that to develop an innovation social networks are required.

Sports innovation requires creative ways to adapt to a changing environment and develop solutions to problems and issues that arise. The group dynamics in sports organizations play a central role in enabling sport innovation. Sports innovation provides structure and value to organizations, individuals and entities involved in sport. Innovative actions are important in the functioning of sports innovation. The sheer economic impact of sport on the economy suggests the importance of innovation. The integration of innovation in sport needs to be better encouraged and understood.

Innovation can be helpful in developing ideas about sport and selling them to others to gain support and commercialize the idea. More work on the context of sport innovation in terms of how opportunities are discovered can add value to knowledge about this area. There has been less work in the innovation literature focusing on sport that examines the effect of context. Innovation might interact with other sport factors so it is important to exploit topics in this area. In sport, the contextual factors of individuals, organizations and teams will affect sport innovation. It is possible that sports innovators have certain personal characteristics that make it easier for them to identify opportunities.

Innovation is both an input and output as it influences creativity in an ecosystem but also the growth of new products or services. Sports innovation is directly relevant to practitioners but due to its interdisciplinary nature research is limited. This is important in providing a more relevant starting point for subsequent studies with sports innovation and related policy implications. Stam (2015:1759) defines ambitious entrepreneurs as "individuals exploring opportunities to discover and evaluate new goods." Ambitious entrepreneurs are important for the development of sports innovations as they see potential when others focus on negative aspects.

Sports innovation

Sports innovation is a term used to describe innovation activities within a sport context. Sports innovation is a vibrant and fresh field of research with promising potential. Innovation is an increasingly popular media term given the emphasis on change in society. However, sports innovation is more than that as it describes innovation activities related to sport. Sports innovation research should explore the idea that innovation can be implemented in a range of sports contexts. Innovation is mostly presupposed to involve risk taking but often innovation involves minor changes that take an imitative approach.

There are two major perspectives of sports innovation. The first one has an emphasis on performance but evaluating the impact of the innovation on improvement. Typically, these types of sports innovations focus on specific quantifiable outcomes such as increase in market share or profitability. The second one focuses on the process of innovation in a sports context. This approach acknowledges that there are positive and negative elements to sports innovation that need to be considered. Some sports have an innovative spirit, such as surfing, and are naturally innovative, whereas others have to work at being innovative, like tennis.

Sports innovation involves the overlapping aspects of sport and innovation by looking at behavior aimed at creating new ideas. Sports innovators attempt to promote ideas while at the same time developing new ideas to create value. It is an inside-out perspective in which an individual, group of people or organization develop specific competences related to sport. The goal of sports innovation is to produce change that serves future demand.

Innovation is a form of futuristic thinking that incorporates ideas not presently seen in the marketplace. The sports innovation mindset involves a style of behavior that is shaped by new ways of thinking. Organizations adopting sports innovation processes identify opportunities in a way to exploit market potential. This involves discovering new forms or additions to existing products and services that emphasize novelty. In order to create sports innovation there needs to be a link between risk management and the leveraging of resources for potential gain. When organizations are involved with innovation they need to evaluate potential while retaining existing products and services. This might mean innovating in a way that captures value by acquiring new knowledge about sport.

Sports innovation is a particular type of innovation that focuses on creativity and the emergence of opportunities. Sports innovation is attractive to businesses and the community, which are interested in new ways of approaching sports-related products and services. This adds clarity to understanding the way innovation affects sport. It also stresses the way sport can be innovative due to its competitive nature. Sports innovation is viewed as combining the established concepts of innovation and sport. In order to tap the full potential of sports innovation there needs to be more focus on the customization of innovation in sport.

The concept of sports innovation is aimed at creating and communicating innovations to sport. An innovative approach to sport involves using novel channels. The new content sports innovation introduces helps keep organizations ahead of the competition. Over the last decade the research focus of sports innovation has evolved significantly in line with technology and societal change. Sports innovation practices have been influenced by the growth in the leisure and technology sectors that have changed the perceptions of sport in the community. Sports innovation has a diverse range of topics utilizing contemporary management practices.

Sports innovation is relevant to practice as a result of the prominence of sport in society. There is a need for more theoretical foundations about sports innovation. Some of the existing work has contributed to shaping the theoretical foundations about sport innovation. There is a need for sports innovation to contribute to knowledge development. This will help to build and maintain credibility about sports innovation. In addition, there is opportunity for sports innovation research to link with practice to optimize output. The mutual dependence between sports innovation research and practice will further support the growth of this field. Sports innovation helps managers deal with the complexities of current and future business trends.

Sports innovation is context dependent due to the environment playing a key role in shaping innovation. Sports innovation can embrace the innovation agenda by combining it with the context of sport. Sports innovation is a psychological process that facilitates transformation of organizations into desired future states. Initiative is needed for sports innovation as there is a degree of creativity with the change process. It is argued that innovation in sport can challenge the status of development in sport. Looking into the future, there is a dearth of innovation research by sports scholars and the simultaneous engagement of theory with practice represents an opportunity.

Sports innovation is a relevant way to understand how sport changes and the role of innovation. Sports innovation works best as it has practical relevance but theoretical grounding. The advantage of taking a sports innovation approach is that it can be utilized to evaluate ongoing efforts of change in sport. Despite the practical significance of sports innovation there is a need to foster more work in this area. This can build on existing work but also focus on new research. Sports innovation will be served greater attention as it is relevant to both practice and theory. Sports innovation research provides a productive means to simultaneously use relevant theories from innovation management applied to sport. Sports innovation is an opportunity that should not be missed as it is important in the business world. Nimrod (2016:390) states "innovation may result from various triggers (internal, external, instrumental or imposed) but is motivation is typically intrinsic." This is linked to the intrinsic motivation for sports innovation because it promotes well-being in sport by creating a way to broaden its role. This helps to give sport a deeper sense of meaning when utilized in an innovative manner.

There is a growing interest in sports innovation due to the understanding that sports need to be imaginative in order to survive. Sometimes there is a lack of knowledge about the link between sport and innovation due to the processes involved. Sports innovation is crucial to the practice of athletes and teams. The performance in sport will depend on responsive strategies around innovation management. Through sports innovation, sport organizations have opportunities to increase their awareness about change and desired outcomes. Barrett and Sexton (2006) propose a generic innovation model that suggests the performance of an innovation is a result of the focus on innovation, which is affected by the context and capabilities for innovation. This generic model is helpful to understand sports innovation as it also comprises the context and capabilities of different sports.

Sports innovation has a profound impact on business and society. Sports innovation can be studied through a variety of disciplines including sport, innovation, psychology, economic geography and sociology. Sports innovation can inform the practice of both innovation and sport. Innovation management has a fragmented body of literature as a result of its interdisciplinary nature and multiple types of innovation that can be studied. Innovation can be divided into technology/production and market/customer types of activities (Abernathy and Clark, 1985). Technology/production innovation refers to the operational processes associated with the development of new products and services. New sport products are increasingly combining technology in how they are produced. Market/customer innovation refers to the distribution of products into the marketplace. More sports products are being developed with customers in a co-creation way.

The mechanisms behind sports innovation need to be understood in greater depth. This involves rethinking the interlink between the sport and innovation disciplines to get a better understanding about interdependencies. This will provide a more holistic picture about the characteristics of sports innovation. A concerted effort to build consensus into what we mean when we talk about sports innovation is required. In this chapter I challenged current conceptualizations of sports innovation by focusing on marketing. It is hoped that the arguments presented in this chapter will lead to a more integrative understanding of sports innovation, which is vital to academics, practitioners and policy discussion.

Conclusion

This chapter has highlighted the increasing interest in knowledge acquisition, dissemination and sharing in sport. Understanding the role knowledge plays in sport can help provide an improved form of sports innovation theory. Sports knowledge can then subsequently be constructed from the theory and practice of knowledge management. As the global economy has increasingly become a knowledge-orientated one, the way sport manages the knowledge process is an important distinctive competitive advantage.

References

Abernathy, W.I. and Clark, K.B. (1985) 'Innovation: Mapping the winds of creative destruction', *Research Policy*, 14(1): 3–22.
Arthur, W.B. (2009) *The Nature of Technology: What it is and How it Evolves*, Free Press, New York.
Assink, M. (2006) 'Inhibitors of disruptive innovation capability: A conceptual model', *European Journal of Innovation Management*, 9(2): 215–233.

Barone, M.J. and Jewell, R.D. (2013) 'The innovator's license: A latitude to deviate from category norms', *Journal of Marketing*, 77(1): 120–134.

Barrett, P. and Sexton, M. (2006) 'Innovation in small, project-based construction firms', *British Journal of Management*, 17: 331–346.

Christofi, M., Leonidou, E., Vrontis, D., Kitchen, P. and Papasolomou, I. (2015) 'Innovation and cause-related marketing success: A conceptual framework and propositions', *Journal of Services Marketing*, 29(5): 354–366.

Foxall, G.R., Goldsmith, R.E. and Brown, S. (1998) *Consumer Psychology for Marketing*, International Thomson Business Press, London.

Funk, D. (2017) 'Introducing a sport experience design (SX) framework for sport consumer behavior research', *Sport Management Review*, 20(2): 145–158

Kraus, S., Harms, R. and Fink, M. (2009) 'Entrepreneurial marketing: Moving beyond marketing in new ventures', *International Journal of Entrepreneurship and Innovation Management*, 11(1): 19–34.

Li, G., Zhang, R. and Wang, C. (2015) 'The role of product originality, usefulness and motivated consumer innovativeness in new product adoption intentions', *Journal of Product Innovation Management*, 32(2): 214–223.

Nimrod, G. (2016) 'Innovation theory revisited: Self-preservation innovation versus self-reinvention innovation in later life', *Leisure Sciences*, 38(5): 389–401.

Orlikowski, W.J. (1992) 'The duality of technology: Rethinking of the concept of technology in organizations', *Organization Science*, 3(3): 398–427.

Ratten, V. (2016) 'The dynamics of sport marketing: Suggestions for marketing intelligence and planning', *Marketing Intelligence and Planning*, 34(2): 162–168.

Ratten, V. and Ferreira, J. (2016) 'Global talent management and corporate entrepreneurship strategy', in Guo, Y., Rammal, H. and Dowling, P.J. (Eds) *Global Talent Management and Staffing in MNEs*, pp. 151–165, Emerald, United Kingdom.

Stam, E. (2015) 'Entrepreneurial ecosystems and regional policy: A sympathetic critique', *European Planning Studies*, 23(9): 1759–1769.

Vargo, S.L., Wieland, H. and Akaka, M.A. (2015) 'Innovation through institutionalization: A service ecosystems perspective', *Industrial Marketing Management*, 44(1): 63–72.

5
CULTURE, SOCIAL AND SUSTAINABLE INNOVATION

Introduction

The purpose of sports innovation has its foundation in culture, people and society because it is more than an economic function as it involves intuition and forecasting demand. The essence of sports innovation is in the application and acceptance of innovation in sport that brings about a change. The outcomes of sports innovation tend to be perceived as positive but there can be no effects or even negative effects as well depending on the circumstances. Having an innovative spirit toward sport enables the joining of old and new management practices. In order to appreciate how innovation can impact on sport it needs to be understood within a societal perspective. This because there is debate about the role of sport in society as a result of both its economic and social position. Therefore, the development of a greater understanding about how sports innovation emerges or is constrained by management inertia that resists the need to change is an area of interest.

Sport is a contest that incorporates a degree of entertainment because of the unknown outcome. The spectacle of sport includes the game but also acknowledges the ceremonial aspect of sport, which is linked to culture. This is seen in the opening and closing ceremonies of the Olympics, which are among the most watched events during the games. Sport is essentially a social experience although the degree of interaction might differ depending on whether the sport is individual or team-based. Some people do not actually play sport but prefer the social activities that go with the sport. For example, many football clubs have social outings that encourage social cohesion rather than the actual playing of sport.

In a sport context, there are physical, psychological and social aspects, which are related to the development of innovation (Ratten, 2012). From a physical perspective, sport offers exercise and a way to improve the health of the human body. Psychologically, sport provides a way to release feelings and stimulate emotional responses. Socially, sport provides a way to connect with others. The different aspects of sport relate to culture and will be dependent on cultural conditions within society.

This chapter touches on the role of culture in sport innovation, which is of great interest to researchers and managers in the course of creating an innovation ecosystem. The nature of culture in a sport context is explored and the interactions between different entities examined. This helps to understand the role of collaboration and trust endemic in cultural conditions that leads to sport innovation.

Culture

The interpretation of sports innovation will vary according to the cultural conditions in a country. Culture involves the social norms and values that are part of behavior in a country but it is hard to define due to its adaptive and shifting nature based on societal change. Morrison (2006:195) states that culture is represented at "different levels (national, regional, business, individual); layers of society (gender, age, social class, occupation, family, religion); and varying context of live (individual, group, community)." Therefore, in a sports context, these different levels play a role in the innovation process.

Culture is a complex phenomenon that involves the collective behavior of a group of people. There has been an increase in the usage of words "entrepreneurial culture" to reflect the changing role of culture within society to be more progressive. Morrison (2006:195) defines an entrepreneurial culture as "an attitude towards commerce at a business level, in which a positive social attitude towards personal enterprise is prevalent, enabling and supporting entrepreneurial activity." As a result of economic turmoil and political uncertainty, more countries are focusing on their entrepreneurial culture, particularly around sport.

There are different ways of using culture to help build sports innovation. This is because some cultures are more collectivist and better at team building, which influences group decision making toward innovation (Christofi et al, 2015). Each sport has a culture based on symbols and identification. Some sports cultures may be more traditional and unwilling to change, which occurs in sports like tennis and football. This is seen in the white clothing most cricketers wear and the policy of white tennis clothing at Wimbledon. However, a particular sports culture might have innovative modes of behavior in terms of how the game is played or off-the-field antics. This means that the fixed sporting codes are fluid and change depending on the sport. As there is often a team-based culture in sport there are social factors influencing innovation. This is seen in famous athletes wearing innovative clothing that is then adopted by other less known or amateur athletes.

There are cultural stereotypes in sport that limit its ability to change. This is seen in tennis players typically considered conservative and from more privileged backgrounds therefore less willing to be innovative. This has changed to a degree with tennis players such as Serena and Venus Williams coming from less privileged backgrounds but being at the top of their sport. In addition, there are different ways of mobilizing and using culture in sport as a form of innovation. This is seen with Serena Williams wearing more colorful clothes than the traditional sportswear worn on tennis courts and having innovative marketing partnerships with Berlei sports bras and OPI nail polish. Other tennis players have also begun innovative sponsorship agreements including Nojak Djokovic with ANZ bank, which is a financial institution not traditionally tied to sports marketing.

Culture is a resource that helps people pursue entrepreneurship. This is because business and educational capital is embedded in cultural values. The attitudes and skills people have that enable them to engage in entrepreneurship come from their cultural background. While there is still debate about whether entrepreneurs are born or made, the knowledge from cultural endeavors helps create specific business entities. This is a result of cultural patterns influencing individual entrepreneurs in the way they behave and act.

Sports innovation ecology

For sports innovation to progress, new ideas need to be demonstrated that have potential to change existing practices. This requires people and organizations having the freedom to experiment and encourage the flow of information. By pushing boundaries of the unknown potential innovations can take shape (Gupta et al, 2016). Innovation incorporates a wide spectrum of activities with sports innovation ecology integrating many different aspects of innovation to present a dynamic view of its relationship to sport. In today's high-velocity competitive landscape it is important to understand holistically the nature of innovation in sport. This a result of innovative developments helping athletes to achieve their goals and generate revenue for business.

Innovation is a buzzword and its effects are evident in most industries but especially those related to sport. Sport organizations have reevaluated the products and services they offer in order to be more innovative. This is the result of increased recognition of the importance of developing a culture of innovation in sports. The long-term survival of sports teams is at the foremost for many sports managers. This is impacted by innovation, which involves the new combination of productive resources. Innovation is a learning process that incorporates using and applying different sources of knowledge. This means that innovation is an interactive process of learning that enables the development of an innovative system.

There has been a move toward understanding innovation as a network of information that is transmitted into knowledge. This involves using information connected to sport to develop innovations and having incentives to introduce new products in sport as people are willing to take risks if it results in an improvement. Sports innovation is often unplanned and happens in a non-linear manner depending on circumstances. Hence, for sports innovation to occur there needs to be a visionary focusing on efforts to bring change into the market. This requires people to focus on innovation as a combined effort between organizations and innovators.

Often networks and networking are used as ways to foster collaboration that is helpful to the emergence of an innovation. Sport innovation tends to have a degree of intuitive understanding of potential market needs. This intuition comes from knowledge about the innovation and how it might develop. Innovation is the key to the survival of sport and its success in the marketplace but is practiced in different ways. For example, small sports clubs might have less sophisticated methods to develop innovations than the more resource-abundant large sport clubs.

Sports innovation is more likely to be dominated by reactions to technology changes and market demand. Once an idea is promulgated then experimentation will take place in order to develop the innovation. Each sport innovation will have its own style depending on the context of its development. Sport has entrepreneurial managers who disregard current practices in order to be proactive about potential opportunities. This is impacted by the entrepreneurial firm who "engages in product-market innovation, undertakes somewhat risky ventures, and is first to come up with proactive innovations" (Miller, 1983: 771). These entrepreneurial sport managers utilize different forms of marketing and resources from social capital to financial investment as a way to develop ideas (Kraus et al, 2009). Entrepreneurial management is defined as "the process by which individuals either on their own or inside organizations pursue opportunities without regard to the resources they currently control" (Stevenson and Jarillo, 1990:23). In a sport context, entrepreneurial managers help develop innovative pathways that bring about change.

Sports innovation management

The culture within a society impacts the degree to which sports innovation is initiated. People living in a society tend to have certain personality traits that affect innovation (Ratten, 2011a). One of the main ways innovation changes the culture of a society is when it involves disruptive change, which transforms the demands and needs of consumers in sport. This leads to a disruption in the former key players of sport in terms of main organizations and their competitive nature. By successfully exploiting a new business model disruptive innovation represents a departure from existing practices (Ratten, 2011b). This helps to bring about fundamental changes in sport and produce unprecedented performance.

The difference with disruptive innovations compared to other types of innovation is that they change how we live. This involves transforming social practices by learning new practices. The significant societal impact of disruptive innovation is the source of future sports innovation. Some sports-related disruptive innovations can be quite risky due to the change they make to the market. In addition, the ambiguous and uncertain effects of disruptive innovations influence development time. In sport, the main types of disruptive innovation involve commercial or technological discontinuity.

Similar to other types of innovation, sports innovation goes through the stages of identifying a problem or issue, developing a solution, planning the development and implementing the idea. These guiding principles of sports innovation help with the exploring of new ideas that may take some experimentation. In order for sports innovation to progress there may be a process of learning and unlearning. This helps to clarify what the innovation is and identify innovation patterns. Often this takes the form of small decision cycles that make up part of the larger decisions around the sports innovation.

Sports innovation results from observing the world differently through the production of new ideas. The emergence of new ideas requires challenging preconceived ideas about what can be done. This enables progressive ideas to come to fruition that involve expanding current market boundaries. Sometimes ambiguous goals will be needed for the sports innovation to gain traction in the market. This will involve changing current thinking models by thinking about previously unknown options about sport. This can help discover unrealized needs in the market that help sport evolve.

In order for a sports innovation to progress there needs to be an interactive process of learning in order to improve outcomes. This means sports innovation acts in a circular way with ideas commercialized then fed back into the market. Sometimes the innovation can be new and trialed in the market rather than waiting until it is perfect. As innovations are important in sport there needs to be this continuous feedback in order to help find the growth of the innovation. For many sports innovations there will be an interdependence between the originator of the idea and feedback from customers about how to progress it. This involves a form of dynamic strategic thinking where the future evolution of the innovation is linked to the original idea.

Learning is a central part of the sports innovation process as there are new developments made by others that affect sport. There are exogenous factors that affect sports innovation including economic, political and social influences, which are important in resource allocation to new ideas. In addition, the competitive structure within an industry affects the development of innovation especially in terms of corporate culture and structure.

Innovation is a hard concept to grasp as it is embedded in a lot of different activities (Assink, 2006). The complex nature of innovation means that it absorbs a lot of time in the development and progressive nature of an idea. This means in order for sports innovation to progress there needs to be a continuous improvement. The capability of the innovators is central in introducing the innovation and subsequently managing its development. Assink (2006:219) refers to the capabilities needed for innovation as being "the key role of strategic management in appropriately adopting, integrating and reconfiguring organizational skills, resources and functional competences to match the requirements of a changing environment." These capabilities are important in sport for generating ideas from multiple sources in order to come up with an innovation.

The ability to accommodate change is important in managing sports innovations as there may be a number of iterations before the successful launch of the idea. Often a sports innovation is outside the current capabilities of an organization, which means they need to develop associated skills to bring the innovation to fruition. The internal driving energy of innovation is in the ability to develop and market effective innovations. This can involve coming up with new concepts that provide an opportunity for business growth.

Sports innovation will quickly gain more attention from researchers and practitioners as a result of its role in sustaining high performance in the sports context. The increased mobility of knowledge workers has enabled the opening up of more innovation opportunities related to sport. This has led to the boundaries of the sports innovation process blurring as the innovation crosses organizational and sector boundaries. Sports innovation is a paradigm that highlights the pervasive nature of innovation in sport.

Sports innovation ideas can be launched from many different sources including within both the professional and amateur sports context. The sports innovations can also go into the market in a variety of ways from social media platforms to international marketing campaigns. The term "sports innovation" is still in its infancy as a result of the confusion in academia about the practical significance of innovation to sport. This has meant that the ideas for sports innovation come from the changes manifested in sports, which have revolutionized the industry.

Initially a lot of the focus on sports innovation has been on the sport itself but this has expanded to related merchandise and technology. Sports innovation connects research from a number of management and marketing fields, which is necessary given the complex nature of sport in different global environments. The emphasis in sport innovation is to organize ideas that have commercial potential but also benefit societal development.

Sports organizations have invested in research and development enabling them to find innovative ideas that have commercial value. The value of sports innovation is immense with many organizations protecting their innovations with intellectual property strategies. This has led to sports innovation being a set of practices emanating from the profiting of innovation in sport. It enables sport to introduce innovation as a way of creating value and interpreting change, which is an important part of the development of sport. Some of these innovations involve spinoff ideas that were a result of changes in an organization.

Spinoffs often come from larger organizations that have a great degree of bureaucracy, which can prevent innovation from flourishing. This has led to spinouts or spinoffs related to sport being established as way to see if an innovation has potential. This is because there are increasing instances of universities and other research institutions partnering with private businesses to explore sports innovations. This can be conducted via selling or donated complements that are part of the sport innovation process. Selling complements involves "accepting commoditization or develop differentiated products based on commodities" (Elmquist et al, 2009:329). This means that sport innovations are sold to other firms as a way to enhance their development. The sport products are then linked to other innovations as a way to broaden their appeal. Donated complements involve "general purpose technologies are sold so users can develop differentiated

TABLE 5.1 Measurement areas of innovation management

Framework	Measurement areas
Commercialization	Sports market research
	Ticket sales, revenue
Innovation strategy	Sport-strategic orientation
	Strategic sports leadership
Inputs	Human capital
	Physical resources
	Finances
Knowledge management	Idea generation
	Process of flow
	Information depository
Organizational elements	Culture
	Management structure
Portfolio management	Ownership
	Communications
	Collaboration
	Efficiency

Source: Adapted from Adams et al (2006).

products (e.g. user toolkits)" (Elmquist et al, 2009:329). This means that the technologies can be innovated to suit the sports context. Both the selling and donated complements are part of the sport innovation process but are also impacted by strategy, inputs and knowledge management. Table 5.1 depicts the main ways that innovation can be measured in a sports context including the framework and areas for development.

User experiences

In order for sport innovations to progress, benefits can be gained from insight into user experiences. Funk (2017:151) states the user experience in sport is conceptualized "as representing a diverse and complex set of two-way interactions across all channels, touchpoints, and time periods during the entirety of the consumer journey that produce cognitive, affective, social and physical responses." The user experience influences the way innovations are adopted to meet customer needs. In addition, user experiences can provide more data and information about how to improve sports services. This is because users become social actors who interact with others as part of the service encounter (Pullman and Gross, 2004).

The user environment for sport will depend on the context and the ability of users to provide suggestions. This includes interactions between users and sport service providers, which enable more improved outcomes based on memorable experiences. This is a result of service encounters; the customer experience is co-created with providers through touchpoints (Vargo and Lusch, 2004). These touchpoints enable a series of interactions to be monitored based on a customer's experience. Funk (2017:151) defines a touchpoint as "all direct and indirect interactions customers experience across multiple channels and at various points in time during the relationship with an organization."

In sport, customer encounters can be on the field or through electronic mediums such as television. There are also unobserved activities as part of sport services that occur before and after games. This means that the customer experience will vary depending on the position in the value chain. In sports, there are sensory elements such as sight and sound that become part of the customer experience. These sensory elements are part of the sports experience amid a competitive landscape. Part of the sensory experience is creating an emotional connection to the sports service. This can be conducted via the compelling and engaging context that creates a unique experience (Pullman and Gross, 2004). Customers often want a sports experience that is consistent so they can obtain the same level of service at multiple venues. This has become important as digital and interactive systems change the customer experience (Funk, 2017).

The World Super 6 is an innovative golf tournament sanctioned by the PGA. It involves changes to conventional golf by having a knockout round and nearest to the pins winners. However, there has been a lack of prize money which has restricted its growth. Golf is trying new things to appeal more to television viewers and increase satisfaction with crowd experiences. In golf, the European Tour has recently proclaimed interest in stadium golf events rather than golf courses. This is a result of sport being on the lookout for innovation due to its need to progress. This involves using imagination to conduct new sports events and experiences. Golf has a tradition of events at existing golf courses but can open up new possibilities.

Sport needs to be creative by allowing imagination to improve games. The embracing of quirky ideas is central to this creativity process that makes sport more interesting. Sport is a business that has changed from being viewed in an amateur manner to being considered a professional activity. In the past, sport was considered a pure leisure activity but the growth in professional sports has changed it to be run in a strategic and business management manner. Some sports innovations, from sponsorship of sports by alcohol companies to online sports betting, bring up some ethical concerns.

Social capital and innovation

In order to understand the process of discovering and evaluating in sports innovation it is helpful to review the role of social capital and network formation. Social capital provides access to social connections that facilitate innovation. The goal of sports innovation is to acquire various social capital that helps to connect the innovation to society. The networks embedded in social capital enable access to economic resources that are conducive to innovation. However, there are power relations in social networks that need to be considered when utilizing social capital. This is due to different people being influenced by the context of the sports innovation, which includes the economic and sociopolitical characteristics.

Social innovation has been gaining momentum as a category of innovation due to its role in creating social and societal equity. Social innovation is evident in sport as a result of the non-profit and amateur aspects of sport. Social innovation focuses on the search for new opportunities that satisfy a social need. These social needs will depend on the contextual factors affecting business and society. In developed countries, the social innovations might focus more on environmental issues but in developing countries the emphasis will be on living standards. Therefore, it is necessary to understand the role sport plays in social change as more innovations focus on this area of market discovery. Innovations that are good for society incorporate new ideas that help solve social problems.

In order for social innovation to develop there needs to be social relationship that focuses on business investment. This enhances society's capacity to be innovative by meeting pressing social concerns. Nicholls and Murdock (2012:7) define social innovation as "varying levels of deliberate change that aim to address sub-optimal issues in the production, availability, and consumption of public goods defined as that which is broadly of societal benefit within a particular normative and culturally contingent context." Phills et al (2008:37) discuss in their definition of social innovation how it differs to entrepreneurship by stating "unlike the terms social entrepreneurship and social enterprise, social innovation transcends sectors, levels of analysis and methods to discover the processes—the strategies, tactics and theories of change that produce lasting impact." In sport, social innovation is important as it encourages linkages between public and private entities.

Sustainability and innovation

Sport is a user of the environment in both positive and negative ways, from the protection of wilderness reserves for hiking and bushwalking to coastlines for surfing and other aquatic activities. However, sport consumes resources from its reliance on water for sports fields to electricity to light up fields. An example of sustainable innovation in sports is Forest Green Rovers, which is a fifth-tier English football team that has a reputation for being eco-friendly. They are based in Southwest England and are a vegan club. In 2017, they applied for planning permission to build the world's first modern-age wooden soccer stadium. The venue will incorporate sustainable practices including green technology. Because a large amount of concrete is used in other sports stadiums, Forest Green Rovers are trying to incorporate design features such as sloping roofs to help the environment. In 2010, the club introduced their green revolution by only serving vegan meals. The club has existing solar panels and an organic pitch.

The importance of sustainability in sport comes from its emphasis on unpredictability as part of its appeal. The unknowing of the result of a sports event is part of the experience. There are a variety of factors influencing this uncertainty in sport including weather, athlete health, coaching performance, the crowd and potential injuries, which all affect sustainability innovations. Increased urbanization, with more people living in cities, has influenced the sports industry. Consumers are becoming more health and fitness conscious and are trying out new sports such as outdoor aerobics. Sports shoes have innovated from being purely used for sport to being everyday shoes worn for lifestyle reasons. This is seen in more colorful and designer sport shoes that have changed from being white to the use of fluorescents and other colors.

Sustainability in sport is influenced by lead user innovation involving people at the forefront of an idea managing the innovation process. Often lead users can change the way an innovation develops by suggesting ways to improve it and linking it to environmental concerns. This involves looking at the information asymmetry between what lead users suggest and how innovation managers can implement this (Kornberger, 2017). Leader user innovation is becoming a more popular, particularly in terms of sport web development, as communities of people get together to propose an idea.

Creating value through sustainability is important in sport. Value co-creation is about the innovation ecosystem that develops from input from business partners, consumers, suppliers and others that help make an innovation (Kornberger, 2017). The co-production of value between the different stakeholders in the co-creation process is useful in a sport context as it typically has a mixture of profit and non-profit entities. Another way co-creation is conducted is through platform innovation, which involves using foundation products, services or technologies as a launch pad for other innovations (Kornberger, 2017). This is helpful with technology innovation that links prior sport products and services together. In sport, some platform innovations will mean that complementary products or services are needed in order to continually innovate. This is important as some sports teams may spend money on implementing a certain platform that can then be used strategically for other services. The interplay between different services on the platform means that it is an important way to strategize for future success. Peer production involves a group of entities sharing the innovation collaboration process. This is helpful in having a pool of common resources that can be utilized to progress a sports innovation.

Conclusion

This chapter has looked into the role of culture and sustainability in sport innovation. Learning about innovation and sport is a way to determine the success of a creative idea but also understand the factors affecting learning. This chapter indicated that engaging with partners for innovation is influenced by cultural factors. Sport innovation tends to need interaction between multiple partners as a way to facilitate innovation. This chapter stresses the need to strategize and think about cultural mechanisms that aim to promote sport innovation.

References

Adams, R., Bessant, J. and Phelps, R. (2006) 'Innovation management measurement: A review', *International Journal of Management Reviews*, 8(1): 21–47.

Assink, M. (2006) 'Inhibitors of disruptive innovation capability: A conceptual model', *European Journal of Innovation Management*, 9(2): 215–233.

Christofi, M., Leonidou, E., Vrontis, D., Kitchen, P. and Papasolomou, I. (2015) 'Innovation and cause-related marketing success: A conceptual framework and propositions', *Journal of Services Marketing,* 29(5): 354–366.

Elmquist, M., Fredberg, T. and Ollila, S. (2009) 'Exploring the field of open innovation', *European Journal of Innovation Management*, 12(3): 326–345.

Funk, D.C. (2017) 'Introducing a sport experience design (sx) framework for sport consumer behavior research', *Sport Management Review*, 20(2): 145–158

Gupta, S., Malhotra, N.K., Czinkota, M. and Foroudi, P. (2016) 'Marketing innovation: A consequence of competitiveness', *Journal of Business Research*, 69: 5671–5681.

Kornberger, M. (2017) 'The visible hand and the crowd: Analyzing organization design in distributed innovation systems', *Strategic Organization*, 15(2), 174–193.

Kraus, S., Harms, R. and Fink, M. (2009) 'Entrepreneurial marketing: Moving beyond marketing in new ventures', *International Journal of Entrepreneurship and Innovation Management*, 11(1): 19–34.

Miller, D. (1983) 'The correlates of entrepreneurship in three types of firms', *Management Science*, 29(7): 770–791.

Morrison, A. (2006) 'A contextualization of entrepreneurship', *International Journal of Entrepreneurial Behavior & Research*, 12(4): 192–209.

Nicholls, A. and Murdock, A. (2012) 'The nature of social innovation', in Nicholls, A. and Murdock, A. (Eds) *Social Innovation*, pp. 1–30, Palgrave Macmillan, Basingstoke.

Phills, J.A., Deiglmeier, K. and Miller, D.T. (2008) 'Rediscovering social innovation', *Stanford Social Innovation Review*, 6(4): 34–43.

Pullman, M.E. and Gross, M.A. (2004) 'Ability of experience design elements to elicit emotions and loyalty behaviors', *Decision Sciences*, 35(3): 551–578.

Ratten, V. (2011a) 'Fundacion Maquipucuna: A entrepreneurial Ecuadorian non-profit organisation', *International Journal of Business and Globalisation*, 6(2): 217–224.

Ratten, V. (2011b) 'Ethics, entrepreneurship and the adoption of e-book devices', *International Journal of Innovation and Learning*, 16(3): 310–325.

Ratten, V. (2012) 'Sport entrepreneurship: Challenges and directions for future research', *International Journal of Entrepreneurial Venturing*, 4(1): 65–76.

Stevenson, H.H. and Jarillo, J.C. (1990) 'A paradigm of entrepreneurship: Entrepreneurial management', in Cuervo, A., Ribeiro, D. and Roig, S. (Eds) *Entrepreneurship: Concepts, Theory and Perspective*, pp. 155–170, Springer, Berlin Heidelberg.

Vargo, S.L. and Lusch, R.F. (2004) 'Evolving to a new dominant logic for marketing', *Journal of Marketing*, 68(1): 1–17.

6
OPEN INNOVATION

Introduction

Sports clubs are more open to innovation due to their flexible structure and connection to other organizations including government bodies and sports federations (Wemmer et al, 2016). Open innovation is a distinct form of innovation in sport, which enables knowledge to flow in and out thereby increasing potential learning outcomes. Value is created through the knowledge flow as it enables sports organizations to harness information from external as well as internal partners. To date, however, it remains unclear how sports innovation is different to other types of innovation. This chapter aims to fill this research gap by investigating the process of open innovation in sport.

Wemmer et al (2016:341) state "innovation can be used as a strategic tool to respond to trends and changes in how sport services are provided and consumed." Innovation is a key driver of long-term success in sports organizations particularly those in global markets. Abecassis-Moedas et al (2016:2842) state "innovation is also an expensive and risky activity, with negative outcomes such as increased exposure to market risk, increased costs, employee dissatisfaction or unwarranted changes." This means that in sport there is often a trial and error approach to innovation that depends on the contextual circumstances.

The presence of innovation in sport has a positive effect on the industry depending on its magnitude and impact. Sports organizations that have the capacity to innovate can more quickly exploit new market opportunities. Sports innovation is particularly important in the early stages of the market, especially where there are new products being developed. In the past decade, several studies have focused on the link between sport and innovation but there has been limited attention due to the early development of sports innovation as a discipline.

Innovation is an exciting area of sports management due to the competitiveness of the global economy and the requirement of creative economic initiatives. Traditionally, innovation has been seen as the end product or output of a process of change (Poutanen et al, 2016). This traditional approach has changed with sports innovation involving a set of behaviors that influence change within a sport context including athletes, clubs, organizations and societies. Therefore, innovation is an important element of sport as a result of its ability to exploit new market opportunities. The main characteristic of sports innovation is in the desire for change and the willingness to make something happen. This is reflected in sports innovators undertaking a number of activities from acquiring resources and recognizing opportunities to completing the tasks.

The structure of this chapter is as follows. First, the role of open innovation is discussed, which postulates that change is a requirement in organizations that increases performance. The role of distributed innovation systems in guiding the sports innovation from idea generation, management of projects to successful outcomes is explained. This helps to link the role of technology in the management of sports innovation. The process of knowledge exchange and dissemination in sport that results in innovation is stated. This helps to enable discussions about the importance of open innovation into a sports innovation context.

Innovation process

Cano-Kollmann et al (2016:259) state that "innovation requires two processes search (the discovery of new knowledge) and transfer (the movement of the knowledge to the point of use)." The search in sports innovation involves looking at new sports and manufacturing technologies as a way to advance the industry. Sometimes the search can happen by chance when utilizing other forms of production in sports. An example is the use of tow in surfing that is popular in big wave conditions. The transfer process involves the person who comes up with the idea translating it into a commercial sense to make it a reality. Often the transfer process involves athletes both past and present who have intimate knowledge of a particular sports product or service.

Sports innovation can be most effectively orchestrated when stakeholders work together to form networks of practice. This is because personal relationships help to create a cohesive environment for innovation to develop. In sport, often there are a limited number of key players that control a sports development so personal relationships are important for the innovation to get into the marketplace (Zaharia et al, 2016). In addition, networking in sport enables relationships to develop that encourage innovation. There is also often a global diaspora of sports fans or prior athletes/coaches that can be accessed as a knowledge source to move forward the innovation. Connected people from a common sports team or sport are important vehicles for affecting innovation. Therefore, the interconnected relationships in sport are a promising way to improve sports innovation processes.

Organizational culture provides the support to encourage an innovation climate in sport. This is important in enabling managers to value innovation and devote resources to it (Assink, 2006). An example of a sports innovator creating a positive organizational culture is Albert Spalding who used technology in the manufacturing of sports equipment. He was originally an athlete, having been a professional baseball pitcher, who then used his knowledge to start manufacturing sports goods.

Culture in an organizational context is defined as "the pattern of arrangement or behavior adopted by a group (society, corporation, or team) as the accepted way of solving problems" (Ahmed, 1998:32). The reality of organizations is that the way things are done determines the culture of innovation (Ahmed, 1998). Often senior sports management needs to support innovation in order to influence how employees behave in an organization. It is hard to define organizational culture in sport due to the complex interpretations of its meaning and application. This is because the term organizational culture is used for "other social groups, ranging from whole nations, corporations, departments and event teams within businesses" (Ahmed, 1998:32).

Culture can be best understood by the intensity and crystallization of it within an organization (O'Reilly, 1989). The intensity refers to the amount of emotions attached to an expectation about certain behavior or values. Some sport cultures have more focused performance and output targets, which affect intensity levels within an organization. Other sport cultures have a relaxed attitude, as they are non-profit or not driven by the need for constant improvement. Crystallization refers to the degree to which behavior is shared among members of an organization. The more people within an organization share the same goals and attitudes, the more cohesive the organizational culture will be.

Open innovation

In open innovation the boundaries are more porous, meaning they absorb the flow of knowledge and information. This is the result of organizations interacting with each other in order to widen their innovative capabilities (Ratten, 2006). As knowledge is a competitive asset, open innovation enables organizations to interact with others instead of recycling internal mechanisms. Knowledge is more widely distributed in society so it is important that organizations focus on knowledge retrieval and sharing of information. The global distribution of knowledge helps accelerate innovations that can be used internally within organizations and for external collaboration.

The ability of organizations to be receptive to new ideas is reflected in their openness to knowledge (Ratten, 2007). The three main dimensions of openness involve innovation sources, degree of reliance on relationships and protection mechanisms (Dahlander and Gann, 2010). The innovation sources refer to the number and quality of external innovation. This is helpful to sports organizations that can utilize knowledge from other sources and industries in the development of their products and services. Degree of reliance on relationships refers to how much knowledge is acquired from partners or network members for innovation. In a sport context, this reliance may be more relevant for non-profit sports organizations that rely on support from government providers. Protection mechanisms refer to how willing other organizations are in allowing access to information in both a formal and informal manner. This is relevant for sports organizations that are structured in a formal manner by hierarchy but that also rely on informal interaction with fans for information.

Organizations can open up their innovation processes by acquiring knowledge and marketing the innovation (Verbano et al, 2015). The acquisition of knowledge can be sourced in a number of different ways from external partners or internal mechanisms within an organization. This exploratory phase is helpful in sports innovation for finding potential ways that might help an organization develop new ideas. The marketing phase involves exploiting the knowledge gained through the exploration stage. This is important as knowledge acquired needs to be put into practice in order for it to have any kind of outcome for an organization.

Open innovation is helpful especially for small sport organizations that may lack financial resources or marketing acumen to put ideas into practice. This means by accessing innovation available in a freely sourced manner the smaller organizations can further commercialize their ideas. Large organizations also benefit from open innovation as they can spread underutilized knowledge. This helps larger organizations to build their network structures in order to capture ideas from emerging firms.

Open innovation is useful for sports organizations to transcend their current market position to come up with new ideas and practices. The environmental uncertainty and the public/private partnerships popular in sport have necessitated a more open approach to considering different approaches. This has led to sports organizations being more progressive about the way they source knowledge. In the open innovation context, innovation can be defined as "the process by which existing knowledge and inputs are creatively and efficiently recombined to create new and valuable outputs" (Felin and Zenger, 2014:915).

It is important to efficiently organize innovation so that it takes into account progressive thinking about sports. This enables a combinative process of linking the benefits of sport to the possibilities of open innovation. The key player in the open innovation process is the sports manager as they govern the way innovation is developed. Sports managers help to foresee potential problem solving and make possible the structural processes needed for open innovation.

Open innovation is a trend in many industries including sports due to the way knowledge can be gained through free exchange of information. There are different degrees of openness from high to low, which influence the level of resulting innovation. There are three major roles that organizations can have in open innovation: funders, generators or market innovators. The role of the funder is to gain monetary resources and in-kind support to enable sports innovations. This might include the use of new materials or technologies in a sports club that are expensive but have a long-term appeal. Generators are those that help come up with ideas and circulate them among a group of people. In sport, the generators can include booster clubs that are linked to professional sports teams. Market innovators are those that see an idea and enable it to be commercialized. In sports this can include new training methods that help build a team's reputation.

Sometimes it is hard to search for innovation, which increases the appeal of open innovation due to the capturing of value being more efficient for the organizations involved. Elmquist et al (2009:330) state "open innovation networks can consist of both deep and wide ties and can be both formal (contractual) and informal." The deep ties refer to how an organization can utilize existing knowledge for innovation. Some organizations will have an abundance of resources including human and social capital that help them find suggestions for possible innovations. This helps utilize existing knowledge without the need to search for new information found in the external environment. Deep ties normally result in more simple or incremental types of innovation. Wide ties refer to an organization's use of outside connections to find new ideas. This involves utilizing external partnerships to help build innovation capacity. Wide ties enable more complex or radical innovations to form.

Part of the emphasis in open innovation is on leadership capabilities that enable people in an organization to be more innovative. Leaders can make decisions such as whether to make or buy products that are needed for innovation. This includes analyzing how to integrate the knowledge within an existing organizational structure. It helps organizations when they make these knowledge decisions in deciding how to exploit information for the best usage. For open innovation to occur there needs to be coordination between entities about innovations. This involves connecting with others in order to find ideas about customer needs and solutions to pressing issues in sport. This may include finding technical solutions to issues addressed by athletes playing sports. A way this is conducted can be through the identification of issues then collaborating with others to find solutions.

Sometimes there needs to be an incentive for sports organizations to collaborate and this can be in the form of government grants. In addition, some knowledge within organizations may be hidden and untapped until others realize its potential. For this reason, encouraging creative usages of existing organizational resources can help build momentum. This leads to the implementation of innovation processes in sports organizations that change the behavior by promoting innovation.

Elmquist et al (2009) suggests that there are three main reasons why an organization will reveal information. First, the information can be used for a purpose closely aligned to the intended usage. This may involve another organization requesting help about a solution that is trade secret although once used has a benefit to both the organizations involved. Open innovation involves using knowledge outside an organization and combining it with internal thought processes. Many ideas for innovation come from outside the organization and are then developed for their own usage (Poutanen et al, 2016). The implementation of ideas from external sources provides a way for sport organizations to utilize innovation developed for other usages but adapt it for the sports context.

Closed innovation involves organizations retaining the knowledge inside their boundaries and keeping intellectual property a secret (Poutanen et al, 2016). The model of closed innovation has changed with more organizations realizing they need to compete but also collaborate. This is evident in the sports industry as there is a need for competition but also for the exchanging of ideas.

Open innovation is defined as "the use of purposive inflows and outflows of knowledge to accelerate internal innovation, and expand the markets for external use of innovation, respectively" (Chesbrough, 2006:1). More sports organizations are utilizing open innovation as a way to change their innovation processes by being more collaborative. This is a result of the innovation process decreasing in productivity due to increased research and development costs. The sharing of knowledge and information through a process of open innovation enables sports organizations to develop better products. This ensures the generation of new revenue streams by leveraging other organizations existing knowledge (Faems et al, 2010). Sometimes organizations have unused ideas that another organization might find useful. Sharing capabilities with other organizations increases the chance that there will be innovation. There are also indirect effects of sharing knowledge that can help to build a sports innovation ecosystem.

Open innovation means that organizations are both active buyers and sellers of intellectual property (Chesbrough, 2012). This is important in the knowledge economy as the key source of competitive advantage for many organizations is their intellectual property. The reason for the increased interest in open innovation is the fact that many organizations are not exploiting their innovations. Many unused patents are blocking or sleeping patents not intended for actual use.

West and Gallagher (2006) suggest four strategies that are important for open innovation: (1) pooled research and development, (2) spinouts, (3) selling complements and (4) donated complements. In sport, the pooling of research and development involves public/private partnerships that enable profit-orientated organizations to collaborate with public institutions. This requires a shift in the sports innovation collaboration process to acknowledge that multiple stakeholders can help with the management of innovation. Spinouts involve related businesses that are set up in partnership with the original organization. This often occurs with non-profit sports organizations setting up commercial ventures. Selling complements refers to products and services that work in tandem with the original innovation. This is also linked to donated complements that involve another organization helping foster the innovation process by providing key inputs.

Distributed innovation systems

Distributed innovation systems have emerged as a way to source new ideas from multiple groups of people and entities. Kornberger (2017:174) states "the hallmark of these distributed innovations systems is that value creation transcends the boundaries of hierarchically organized firms." This is a result of modern organizations changing to include multiple groups of organizations that need to work together for innovation outcomes. More work is going into designing systems that work outside organizational boundaries as well as within them.

There are a number of different types of distributed innovation systems from co-creation, crowdsourcing, platform innovation and user-driven innovation (Kornberger, 2017). The increase in interest in distributed innovation systems comes from the increased usage of technology in society that reduces communication costs (Langlois and Garzarelli, 2008). Technology has helped to provide an easier way to search for information that leads to innovation. This is important in identifying new opportunities for sports innovation and creating a viable business solution. Organizations are now more efficient at transmitting information to third parties as a way to maximize innovation. There is also increased emphasis on knowledge sharing as a result of the information infrastructure and data analysis used by organizations.

More people use a wide variety of technology devices that encourage an interconnected system of knowledge. Lakhani and Panetta (2007:98) refer to information systems in their definition of distributed innovation as "decentralized problem-solving, self-selected participation, self-organizing coordination and collaboration, 'free' revealing of knowledge and hybrid organizational models that blend community with commercial success." The benefit of the distributed innovation process is that it enables connection between users, organizations and competitors (Kornberger, 2017).

Sport innovators are able to come up with new ideas and usages for sports-related products and services. New technology has resulted in a change in the way people consume sport. This has also been in conjunction with more people being interested in sport as a form of physical activity but also leisure activity. The understanding of sports innovation management is important in all sports context, including amateur, professional, not-for-profit, government and international. This is a result of the determination of how to use human, financial and intellectual resources being at the core of sports management functions. Therefore, it is important for sport managers to monitor developments and trends in the industry in order to foster knowledge sharing but also be involved in innovation. In order to produce better products and services there needs to be more emphasis on sports innovation. New forms of sports have become popular in recent years due to the increased emphasis on risk taking and integrating new forms of technology.

In sport there have been mechanisms to reduce the success of one team by including salary caps that aim to distribute talent among teams. The NFL draft is a televised event and there are regulations in terms of which team picks the first player in order to produce more equal competition. In addition, there are age restrictions in the NFL that limits the number of available players. This creates a more level playing field—different to other businesses where often certain organizations are allowed to dominate the market.

Sports and technology innovation

Sports innovation is a broad concept that includes a number of different dimensions such as the combination of good ideas for sport with an instinctive understanding of what is needed. Good ideas in sport can range from commercial, design, manufacturing, management and technical activities. In older sports, innovation can offer new ways of delivering value to established and mature sports. This is seen in barefoot bowls at lawn bowling clubs that encourage younger people to play a sport that has traditionally been for older members of the community. In newer sports such as surfing, there has been the introduction of non-zip wetsuits by Rip Curl that are more flexible to wear as well as the use of quick-dry technology.

Innovation is an imperative foundation of a sports organizations competitive advantage. The synergistic energy of innovation can provide sports organizations with a competitive advantage. However, sports organizations need to manage the innovations they sell and market to consumers. They can do this through sport service organizations including fitness centers, golf clubs and ticket sale operators. In a sport context, this means innovation can occur on the field, in the locker room, on television or through a variety of other ways. However, the nature of the innovation may depend on the demographics, with younger consumers of sports products being natural innovators. Indeed, they are called digital natives as technology has been a part of their life since birth. This demographic segment has been early adopters of electronic gaming and other technological innovations in sport.

Electronic sport (e-sport) is innovative as it enables the use of information and communications technology as part of a mental or physical activity. E-sport is also watched by fans who see people playing e-games. This has led to the development of live streaming and e-games events at sports stadiums. E-games are innovative in both a competitive sense and a commercial sense as people can follow the game in an e-format. This new form of sport has unique characteristics, as it is more orientated to mental activities rather than physical activities. Despite the lack of physical activity e-sport is still highly sought after by consumers.

Sport and society

The concepts of innovation and sport are somewhat indivisible due to the interlinkages between each as a form of behavior. Innovation is a tool in sport as it enables the exploitation of change. A recent innovation in sports apparel is the focus on the female market. The NFL has a special line of female clothing and the Australian Football League recently launched a women's league. Often sport teams have a long connection to the community so increasing gender diversity in sport is a way to expand their markets. In addition, the historical and geographical position of many sports teams leads them to be integrated within the community. Therefore, the community spirit toward a sport team enables innovative ways of support. This may be in the form of signage or products linked to the local sports team.

Sport has gained from innovation reinvigorating the industry and improving performance by coming up with better ideas and usages. Often sport is an inherent part of a person's identity and people feel like they are part of a sporting community. This is seen in adventure sports with people associating with the lifestyle of the sport. For example, rock climbing is mostly in outdoors areas, including national parks, so people playing this sport are likely to also enjoy the natural environment. However, indoor rock climbing is an innovation and has been developed for people in an indoor setting that is more likely to be in urban areas. Other sports are more team-based and people often feel a sense of comfort in being part of a club. This is evident in team sport membership rates and group activities. There is also the socialization aspect that encourages people who like a sports team to be part of the team experience in other ways. For example, in college football in the United States, cheerleaders and musicians are part of the sports teams.

Sport has become more professional based with an increase in sport managers, agents and coaches who are integrated into management functions. Innovative sports initiatives tend to incorporate technological innovation and increased competition for revenue. This is the result of sport being a combination of multiple activities related to the game, including entertainment, merchandise sales and online commentary. Both profit and non-profit sports entities have adopted an innovative approach to the management of sport in order to increase market opportunities.

Voluntary and non-profit sport organizations have become more similar to profit-orientated sports organizations due to changes in funding requirements. Within both forms of sport there are participation and spectator services that incorporate innovation. Participation sport services involve individuals playing, umpiring or refereeing sports events. Sport referees are increasingly using technology to help them with play decisions. Despite this technological advantage for referees in helping them make decisions there is still the desire for human connection in sport. Spectator services involve watching sports events and can be direct such as physically being at a game or indirect such as sports betting or fantasy sports games.

Sports and innovation problems

Innovation problems can be classified as complex or simple (Felin and Zenger, 2014). Complex problems "involve a vast array of highly interdependent elements, choices, and knowledge sets that must be creatively recombined to compose valuable solutions" (Felin and Zenger, 2014:916). In a sport context, complex problems involve different parts and issues that are hard to understand. This may mean athletes needing better equipment that incorporates new technology. Or it could involve the interaction of athletes on sports fields that have a sustainability initiative to them. In order to understand complex problems it helps to focus on the knowledge needed to solve the relevant issue. There can be a variety of solutions that need more distinct knowledge that only specialized sports people know. Alternatively the knowledge can involve the intuition of sports people on what may work, based on their experience and available resources.

Simple problems are easy to solve as a result of the shorter time needed to make a decision. Often feedback based on trial and error will make a problem easier to solve (Felin and Zenger, 2014). In sports organizations there may be a need to get a broad set of people together to solve simple problems. This is because there is an interdependence among people in terms of input that can help solve a problem in sport.

In sport, there is a sense of tradition that is embraced but at the same time other elements, such as playing clothes, may be more modern. Innovation is the main driver for many sports brands, including Lululemon who provide a free yoga lesson in their stores as way to attract customers. With sports products there is little price resistance and consumers are willing to pay for innovation. Lululemon has incorporated lightweight fabrics and new prints, patterns and textures in their clothing. Lululemon markets itself as a community rather than just a company by engaging with customers. Moreover, Lululemon have introduced new store formats, including the Lululemon Lab in New York that splits the space between retail and a designer studio.

Conclusion

This chapter has discussed the role of open innovation in sport. This is becoming increasingly important as more organizations utilize open innovation as a way to co-create solutions to existing problems and prioritize future capabilities. In addition, open innovation is linked to technological change, which is at the forefront of the sports industry. This will lead to more focus on the role of sport in society and the influence of technology.

References

Abecassis-Moedas, C., Sguera, F. and Ettlie, J.E. (2016) 'Observe, innovate, succeed: A learning perspective on innovation and the performance of entrepreneurial chefs', *Journal of Business Research*, 69(8): 2840–2848.

Ahmed, P.K. (1998) 'Culture and climate for innovation', *European Journal of Innovation Management*, 1(1): 30–43.

Assink, M. (2006) 'Inhibitors of disruptive innovation capability: A conceptual model', *European Journal of Innovation Management*, 9(2): 215–233.

Cano-Kollmann, M., Cantwell, J., Hannigan, T.J., Mudambi, R. and Song, J. (2016) 'Knowledge connectivity: An agenda for innovation research in international business', *Journal of International Business Studies*, 47(3): 255–262.

Chesbrough, H. (2006) *Open Innovation: The New Imperative for Creating and Profiting from Technology*, Harvard Business Press, Cambridge, MA.

Chesbrough, H. (2012) 'Open innovation: Where we've been and where we're going', *Research Technology Management*, 55(4): 20–27.

Dahlander, L. and Gann, D.M. (2010) 'How open is innovation?', *Research Policy*, 39(6): 699–709.

Elmquist, M., Fredberg, T. and Ollila, S. (2009) 'Exploring the field of open innovation', *European Journal of Innovation Management*, 12(3): 326–345.

Faems, D., de Visser, M., Andries, P. and Van Looy, B. (2010) 'Technology alliance portfolios and financial performance: Value-enhancing and cost-increasing effects of open innovation', *Journal of Product Innovation Management*, 27: 785–796.

Felin, T. and Zenger, T.R. (2014) 'Closed or open innovation? Problem solving and the governance choice', *Research Policy*, 43: 914–925.

Kornberger, M. (2017) 'The visible hand and the crowd: Analyzing organization design in distributed innovation systems', *Strategic Organization*, 15(2): 174–193.

Lakhani, K.R. and Panetta, J.A. (2007) 'The principles of distributed innovation', *Innovations*, 2(3): 97–112.

Langlois, R.N. and Garzarelli, G. (2008) 'Of hackers and hairdressers: Modularity and the organizational economics of open-source collaboration', *Industry and Innovation*, 15(2): 125–143.

O'Reilly, C. (1989) 'Corporations, culture and commitment: Motivation and social control in organizations', *California Management Review*, 31(4): 9–25.

Poutanen, P., Soliman, W. and Stahle, P. (2016) 'The complexity of innovation: An assessment and review of the complexity perspective', *European Journal of Innovation Management*, 19(2): 189–213.

Ratten, V. (2006) 'Policy drivers of international entrepreneurship in Europe', *EuroMed Journal of Business*, 1(2): 15–27.

Ratten, V. (2007) 'Organisational learning: How can it foster alliance relationships?' *Development and Learning in Organisations: An International Journal*, 22(1): 20–21.

Verbano, C., Crema, M. and Venturini, K. (2015) 'The identification and characterization of open innovation profiles in Italian small and medium-sized enterprises', *Journal of Small Business Management*, 53(4): 1052–1075.

Wemmer, F., Emrich, E. and Koenigstorfer, J. (2016) 'The impact of coopetition-based open innovation on performance in non-profit sports clubs', *European Sport Management Quarterly*, 16(3): 341–363.

West, J. and Gallagher, S. (2006) 'Challenges of open innovation: The paradox of firm investment in open source software', *R&D Management*, 36(3): 319–331.

Zaharia, N., Kaburakis, A. and Pierce, D. (2016) 'Sport management programs in business schools: Trends and key issues', *Sport Management Education Journal*, 10: 13–28.

7
CORPORATE ENTREPRENEURSHIP

Introduction

Sport has received scant attention in the corporate entrepreneurship literature, particularly with respect to the development of innovation. This neglect is unfortunate as there is more emphasis on sport ventures as a form of corporate entrepreneurship. Sport represents a distinct way strategic ventures can be conducted that integrates innovative thinking. This means that deliberately linking corporate entrepreneurship into sport provides a valuable way to understand the effects of innovation. Therefore, corporate entrepreneurship may offer appealing ways to study sports innovation management. It is hoped that this chapter will contribute to filling the gap between corporate entrepreneurship and sports innovation management.

Most of the existing sport management research is focused on one disciplinary area with little connection to other disciplines (Gerrard, 2015). This has led to there being lost opportunities from the little overlap between research about corporate entrepreneurship, innovation and sport management. Sport is an industry "composed on a market or recreational and competitive users, manufacturers of equipment, suppliers of services, and complementary goods and services" (Thomas and Potts, 2016:566). Critical understandings about innovation can enhance sport management by valuing entrepreneurial behaviors. In this chapter I argue that sport scholars need to pay more attention to the work in the field of corporate entrepreneurship.

Despite the important role corporate entrepreneurship plays in the construction of sport innovation, there has been relatively little critical work focused on innovation in sport organizations. This has resulted in there being less attention paid to how innovation in sport organizations uses corporate entrepreneurship to produce creative results. Sports innovation has its roots in both physical education and entrepreneurship, both of which focus on competitiveness. Knoppers (2015:498) states "being a leader in a sport organization may mean taking on values embedded in popular discourses about sport and about corporate life." This linkage between corporate entrepreneurship and sport is further investigated in this chapter.

Sport organizations are not a homogenous group as they differ in size, location and capabilities. For the sport industry to be innovative organizations need to support corporate entrepreneurship initiatives. Sport operates in a complex and multi-faceted environment that is driven by competitive pressure and sport organizations can revise their businesses by internally developing new products or services. This can be done via acquisitions and alliances with other firms in order to increase knowledge acquisition that leads to new product development. Zahra (1991:261) states "these innovative managerial practices can take place at almost every functional area within the corporation, with the intent of creating momentum to increase innovations in products or markets." Thus, corporate entrepreneurship is linked to innovation as it enables the seizing of opportunities in the market.

There has been little attention given to corporate entrepreneurship and how it is utilized by sports leaders in organizations. There have been few sport scholars who have taken up the task of embedding corporate entrepreneurship within sport. This needs to be done as there are more business aspects to sport than there were in the past. This has meant the transformation of amateur sports clubs to commercialized ones is a byproduct of a corporate entrepreneurship strategy.

The role of sport organizations is changing as they need to focus more on corporate strategy to be competitive. This has resulted in more pressure on sport organizations to be entrepreneurial and diversify their income away from government funding. The main entrepreneurial competences that are important for organizations to develop are conceptual thinking, opportunity recognition, organizing, problem-solving skills and strategic competences (Man et al, 2002). These skills are part of the competences needed for corporate entrepreneurship. This means that sport organizations need to develop better ways to organize ideas that are derived from conceptual thinking as a form of strategic advantage. This can involve recognizing opportunities before other organizations do as a way to solve problems in the industry. Successful sports organizations need to believe in their ability to control business ventures as a form of corporate initiative. This can include sport organizations that manage their businesses with the intention of expanding that business in the future.

There are a variety of different types of corporate sport entrepreneurs. Most focus on deriving economic or financial gain from sport businesses. Although some of these corporate entrepreneurs recognize the need to balance economic goals with environmental and social needs. Traditionally sport organizations have focused on corporate activities they derive financial value from but this is changing with more interest in balancing business and community interests in the form of corporate social responsibility.

In this chapter, the relevance of corporate entrepreneurship to sport is discussed. This provides background to the role corporate ventures and strategic entrepreneurship play in sport. The chapter provides suggestions for the future of sports and corporate entrepreneurship by seeking to explore the role of sport business in society by taking an innovation perspective. By doing so it considers sport as innovative and that managers of sport can involve other stakeholders in decisions. This enables an understanding about how sport can be used for business purposes because of its innovative nature and emphasis on corporate entrepreneurship.

This chapter is structured into three major sections. The next section reviews the development of sport as a business, culminating in the use of corporate entrepreneurship theory as a theoretical framework. The following section presents the ways sport and business are linked in meaning in terms of their focus on corporate ventures and strategic planning, which are part of corporate entrepreneurship. The final section discusses the role of sport business has in innovation ecosystems and global networks.

Sport organization

Smith and Westerbeek (2007:3) define a sport organization as "advancing towards profit or non-profit objectives that involve sport participation or spectator services." Sport business involves analyzing the interests of the community, consumers, environment, investors and suppliers in decisions about sport. There is a link between sport and business due to the emphasis on performance but also because of the variety of functions that sports entities are involved in. This is seen in the suggestion that executive leaders are a form of corporate athlete as they need to look after their mind, body and spirit. Therefore, sport bridges economic and social gaps in society that encourage a collaborative approach to business.

There are six key stakeholder groups that are relevant to organizations: business partners, communities, customers, employees, environment and investors. Business partners in sport take a variety of forms depending on the context. Some are competitors while others are government or non-profit entities. This has led to the term "coopetition" being popular in the sports context as organizations both collaborate and compete with each other. In sport, communities can be either geographically or emotionally based depending on whether they are located near a sports area or are part of an online group. Increasingly due to the combined nature of physical and spectator sport with technological advancements such as analytics, there is an interplay between location and online communities. There are electronic gaming communities in addition to fan-based communities that all encourage the sharing of information and knowledge around a specific sport. In addition, fantasy sport has increased in popularity as a result of the ability of fans to choose their own players and play in an online environment. Customers in sport can include people, business and governments. These customers influence the types of services a sport entity offers and the prices paid for these services. There are also different types of consumers from loyal supporters of a sports club to transient customers who support sports teams based on their performance. Employees are paid workers of sports organizations. There are also a large number of volunteers in sports organizations that are unpaid. The environment is important for sport as the outdoors is often the natural amphitheater of events. Lifestyle sports such as walking are in natural environments. Investors in sport include members of sports clubs or private companies interested in a financial role. All these stakeholders contribute to the development of an entrepreneurial ecosystem in sport.

Sport and entrepreneurship

The link between innovation and entrepreneurship is evident in many studies because innovation can result in entrepreneurship. This is evident in entrepreneurship being carried out through innovation, strategic renewal and business ventures. Sahut and Peris-Ortiz (2014:665) state "not only does innovation appear as an inherent characteristic of entrepreneurship but innovation and entrepreneurship must go hand in hand." Therefore, the need for innovation in sport makes the concepts of sport and innovation converge in management practices. The conditions for innovation in sport do not always require money or need close cooperation from a group of people and organizations. This involvement ensures the sports innovation is unique and different to existing practices. Sports needs innovation dynamics to ensure there is commitment among a group to ensure the knowledge is transferred into commercial practice. This can include the sports innovation partners having the motivation to provide a benefit to the sports community through both financial and non-financial means.

There are both personal and social conditions that influence the practice of sports innovation. The personal conditions are individual characteristics and psychological, which is evident in sports players coming up with their own innovations. These personal conditions can result in many athletes going into business despite competition being their passion. Many ex-athletes excel in business as a result of their competitive nature, their desire to win and also, in many instances, their sporting experiences in a collaborative environment. Many professional athletes are experienced in working with a diverse range of people and can utilize their marketing experience in a business context. Moreover, the intuition that has helped athletes perform on the sports field can be used in a business setting to develop innovation. Other personal characteristics relate to demographics such as age, sex and professional experience. The social conditions are based on cultural, environmental and institutional factors, which affect innovation in sport. This is seen in some environments such as amateur sports leagues having strong connections to the local community, which instills an ability to utilize social networks for innovative purposes.

Sport and innovation

The interaction of sport as an innovation requires the presence of collaborative values that lead to more supportive business ventures. Sports innovation activity can increase when there is a more favorable social environmental that includes less fear of failure and better understanding of the innovation process. Sports innovation is determined by the set of social norms existing in society that effects behavior. The social interactions between individuals and social groups have consequences for sports innovation activity and are linked to the entrepreneurial nature of the sports industry.

Garner et al (2016:198) state "the sport industry has the longest continuous running history of statistics to measure performance." These statistics have recently been referred to as data analytics due to their ability to examine sports performance using different approaches. The performance of sports teams or athletes can be measured in a variety of ways and this requires a complex understanding of how certain actions lead to performance. Ways to measure sports performance occur at the individual, management and team level. In addition, there is incentive pay in sport that is often based on performance outcomes. This has led to there being both similarities and differences found in the innovation management and sports business literature, and to an expectation that by combining both the innovation and sports literature our understanding of sports innovation management can be broadened.

Sports innovation can provide research with practical impact due to its importance in society and related sectors. Gerrard (2015:506) states "sport management is 'management in context' and context is vital to effective research-based interventions." This means that there are diversities in approach to sport management as a result of the multiple areas of study. In addition, there are numerous alternative ways to measure innovation in sport. For example, innovation can be in the introduction of new sports products but also in the way a game is managed. This leads to sports innovation being a multi-faceted concept that requires a holistic understanding about its application. The growing interest in innovation in sport offers vast opportunities for both sport and management scholars.

A practice-based innovation is the introduction of radical restructuring in coaching and playing staff by Saracens, a rugby union club (Gerrard, 2015). This was a form of sport innovation as it changed the way rugby union was played and managed in order to create better market performance. Sport innovation is a result of knowledge co-production that melds information dissemination with knowledge creation. Gerrard (2015) discusses the process of knowledge co-production in a sports context as it bridges academic and user perspectives. This is due to sports innovation being a transformational process that enables knowledge to be shared in a range of settings.

Sports innovation management draws from other business disciplines as the combination between sport and innovation makes it distinctive. There is an inherent diversity in sports innovation that incorporates the goal of focusing on a niche area but having practical relevance. The benefit of sports innovation is that it has significance beyond just a sports context as it incorporates innovative management practices.

The most significant role of innovation in sport is in creating a more meaningful way to enjoy it. Often the impact of sports innovation is in creating an environment conducive to opportunities that promotes better societal wellbeing. This has meant that there is a pressing need to develop a comprehensive understanding of the dynamic nature of innovation in sport. This involves analyzing the processes, resulting business ventures and the outcomes of sports innovation. This represents an important step toward the development of a sports innovation theory. For sports innovation to be successful there needs to be an innovation champion that obtains the resources and manages the ideation process. The way to strengthen the innovation capacity in a sports context is important and requires the facilitation of an innovation champion.

Innovation in a broad sense involves new learning that occurs when combinative capabilities are produced from existing knowledge (Troilo, 2014). To stay competitive sports organizations need to reorder inputs in creative ways. This may involve the use of knowledge in a new combination that involves novel findings. The need to innovate is prevalent in sport due to the competitiveness endemic in the industry. It is hoped that fostering innovation in sport will fuel economic development but the innovation needs to involve unexplored potentials that involve knowledge usages.

There are many reasons why sport organizations are involved with innovation but the primary objective is to increase profitability. The ability to learn is a key feature of the innovation process and this is referred to as absorptive capacity. Absorptive capacity means that an organization will learn from another entity about new knowledge that is then used for productive purposes. The foundation of successful use of absorptive capacity is in the recombination of knowledge.

Clark (2009:215) states that innovation involves "the transposition of a product, process or practice to a new context with beneficial commercial results." In order to have real applications, sports innovation needs to include new products, processes or technologies. Sports innovation has the capacity to commercialize ideas that were developed in both an amateur and professional sports context. This is because sports organizations need to integrate the innovation into other support structures that can leverage their experiences. Innovative sport organizations normally have experience outside sport that provide a sense of interdependence between sport and the innovation process. Innovative sports managers generally are more willing to take calculated risks because of their ability to tap into their social networks. The enables innovative sports managers to use their imagination and enthusiasm to get the idea to fruition. This is important as some innovations may need to be adapted and the process requires a degree of determination and patience.

In sport, there is an orientation toward achievement that enables the development of innovations. Often sports innovators need to be optimistic and self-confident about developing an idea as it takes hard work. In sport, there is a more sympathetic environment to innovate because of the experience in winning and losing. Thus, the sports environment makes innovations more likely as both private and non-profit organizations can collaborate.

The significance of innovation to sport is highlighted by the large organizations and teams investing in new technologies. Individual governments have also stressed the significance of sport innovation by promoting creative solutions to existing problems. Shah (2005), in a study of boardsports industries (skateboarding, snowboarding and windsurfing), discussed how everyday innovations can lead to discoveries through use. This means that the social interactions people have in sports leads to new ways of doing things. Moreover, sport innovates through modifying equipment in order to provide better outcomes.

Sporting goods have been innovative as they use engineering and technology advancements (Thomas and Potts, 2016). The extreme sports industry has been the recipient of many innovations that have enabled risk-taking ideas to find an audience. This is evident in the development of rodeo kayaking, which grew from user innovations (Hienerth, 2006). Rodeo kayaking or freestyle kayaking involves "a branch of white water kayaking that where the paddler performs various technical moves and tricks in one place (a playspot)" (Thomas and Potts, 2016:575). Rodeo kayaking thus is a combination of two sports: rodeo and kayaking, which have emerged to create an innovative sport. Although few people know about rodeo kayaking it provides an interesting example of a new sport being developed from an innovative idea.

Corporate entrepreneurship

There are debates about how to define entrepreneurship but it involves a number of behaviors including innovation, initiating, maintaining, risk and strategy (Hurley, 1999). A basic definition of entrepreneurship is "the pursuit of opportunity without regard to the resources currently controlled" (Stevenson, 1983:1). A broader definition of entrepreneurship is "the environment conditioning opportunity, the process of discovering opportunity, the evaluation and exploitation of opportunity and the individual decision makers who do these things" (Roomi and Harrison, 2010:152). In the sport context, there are incentives to being entrepreneurial due to the resources endemic in sport that provide access to information about potential business opportunities. The establishment of sports enterprises not only contributes to economic and political development but also provides a way for social goals to be realized.

Entrepreneurship is about change but it incorporates creation of new ventures (Bruyat and Julien, 2000). Bruyat and Julian (2000) suggest that there are four main types of entrepreneurship: entrepreneurial reproduction, imitation, valorization and ventures. Entrepreneurial reproduction involves "very little new value creation, usually no innovation and very few changes for the individual" (Bruyat and Julien, 2000:173). This means that ideas about changes in sport can transfer from one geographic location to another. The idea is new but it is essentially the reproduction of an idea from another source. Another example is a football player who has made his own sporting gear going into business for themself. Essentially they are doing the same thing but in an entrepreneurial manner that incorporates a business venture.

Entrepreneurial imitation involves no significant new value creation but utilizes know-how for the business idea (Bruyat and Julien, 2000). In order to develop sports innovation, organizations utilize corporate entrepreneurship as a business strategy. Sports innovation is influencing the way sport is conducted and making creativity an imperative in the industry. Corporate innovation is defined when "individuals in an established firm pursue entrepreneurial opportunities to innovate without regard to the level and nature currently available resources" (Kuratko, 2016:477). Corporate innovation is different to corporate entrepreneurship as it emphasizes change but not business creation.

Corporate entrepreneurship is important in the sports context as businesses need to embrace new ideas that can potentially lead to better performance. The existence of an innovation strategy in sport means that there is a strategic intent to continuously focus on change. Some sports organizations do this by focusing on corporate entrepreneurship as a way to take advantage of opportunities when they first emerge. This willingness to embrace change is a way sports organizations can enhance existing services by providing improvements. Integrating corporate entrepreneurship into a sports organization's mission and values statement is an important way of fostering the innovation process.

There are three main types of corporate entrepreneurship: creation of new businesses, renewing existing businesses and changing competition rules (Stopford and Baden-Fuller, 1994). The creation of new businesses is sometimes referred to as corporate venturing or intrapreneurship (Stopford and Baden-Fuller, 1994). This is important in large sport organizations that have an abundance of resources but need to be creative about its use. By coming up with new businesses both profit and non-profit sports organizations can keep up to date with potential changes in the industry. This helps reduce risk by planning for future needs and opportunities. The renewal of existing businesses involves transforming them into more productive resources. In sport, this often occurs when new products such as shoes are relaunched through innovative marketing campaigns. Alternatively it can mean focusing on the sport organization's brand recognition by going into areas that were previously under resourced.

The changing of competition rules enables sports organizations to enter new international markets. This is helpful with new technology that might alter the way sport is viewed. All types of sports entrepreneurship are based on innovation that enables new possibilities. Sports entrepreneurship can occur when extra capabilities are created or resources deployed for new reasons. This can result in a wide range of outcomes for sports organizations including the establishment of new ventures.

Entrepreneurship that is game changing involves producing something significantly different to what has been done previously by transforming an organization

(Stopford and Baden-Fuller, 1994). In order for sports to utilize entrepreneurship there needs to be a team-orientation that involves a group of people working together. Teams can build coalitions to support innovation by encouraging better information dissemination and decision making. Team members need to act as independent entities to encourage creativity but also work together with others toward a group goal. This means that there needs to be an awareness about the tendency to groupthink that can bias decisions. Groupthink often occurs when people get together to discuss innovation as some individuals may want to please the group rather than focus on their own thoughts. Groupthink often occurs in sports teams as athletes dress the same and are encouraged to act in the same manner. Although this is changing there is still a tendency to be members of a group in sports teams than individual entities with different behaviors.

As part of teamwork there are also tasks that need to be delegated, which involves a degree of bureaucracy (Stopford and Baden-Fuller, 1994). Despite this sense of bureaucracy there can be some flexibility in the way tasks are designed. After a team has been set up there needs to be a focus on learning as a way to induce innovation. This can occur when individuals in a team explore new ideas. A degree of inertia may exist in teams that are reluctant to learn about different possibilities and options to change.

Corporate entrepreneurship provides a way of re-energizing sports organizations that have outdated modes of behavior. This includes both formal and informal activities that lead to creation of new businesses in existing organizations. To be considered entrepreneurial the organizations need to focus on market initiatives in sport. Sharma and Chrisman (1999:18) define corporate entrepreneurship as "the process whereby an individual or a group of individuals, in association with an existing organization, create a new organization or instigate renewal or innovation within that organization." This definition is adopted in this chapter as a way of understanding the role of corporate entrepreneurship in sport facilitating the innovation process.

In order to achieve corporate entrepreneurship there needs to be an organizational environment conducive to innovation. Hornsby et al (2002) suggest that there are five ways to ensure this innovative environment exists for influencing manager's entrepreneurial behavior and they are: (1) management support, (2) work discretion/autonomy, (3) rewards/reinforcement, (4) time availability, and (5) organizational boundaries. Management support involves the role of leaders in supporting innovation within organizations. For sports innovation to develop there needs to be top management support in order to provide resources and coordinate staff. Some professional sports organizations are able to devote more time and money toward innovation. Work discretion/autonomy involves the ability to provide flexibility and tolerance of new ideas that might fail then be resurrected. This is important in helping with delegating responsibility to tasks that help provide better commitment to innovation. Some athletes have the discretion to change their clothing or equipment if in line with regulations, which might involve a degree of user innovation.

Rewards/reinforcement involves recognizing good ideas and helping ensure they come to fruition. Part of this process might include focusing on achievements and encouraging people to persevere in times of hardship. Sometimes there may be challenges in managing the sports innovation so it is important to have support. Time availability means giving people the freedom to devote time to creative tasks. This can be in the form of having an easier workload to ensure more strategic innovations occur. Creativity can also be fostered when there is a designated time to conduct thinking and strategic planning exercises. Organizational boundaries involve explaining to others about how the sports innovation will evolve. This is important in ensuring that expectations are communicated to people participating in the sports innovation. To ensure the development of successful sports innovation there needs to be knowledge about the process and rules of engagement. This ensures that an organization can develop an innovation-facilitating mechanism that works in harmony. Part of this process is managing failures that often occur as part of the innovation process before a successful innovation takes place.

Shepherd and Kuratko (2009) discussed how it is important to manage grief about failures in order to enhance learning about innovative projects. Corporate entrepreneurship will often involve failures but the ability to learn and grow from these failures is an important skill. There can be different ways people and organizations manage the failures from corporate entrepreneurship including acknowledging that failures are part of the innovation process. However, for some organizations the management of failures needs to be analyzed in terms of costs and benefits. In sport there are new products and technologies that are developed only to be not accepted in the marketplace. Hence, there is a degree of trial and error in terms of developing new sports innovations.

For corporate entrepreneurship to succeed it needs to incorporate the hardware and software side of organizations. Kuratko (2016:486) states the "hardware side of organizations (strategy, structures, systems and procedures) is the contextual framework within which individuals take their behavioral cues." This means that having the right procedures for innovation to develop in sport is important. Some organizations might have specific guidelines people need to follow about innovation. This can include intranet facilities that enable sharing information in an organization. Kuratko (2016) contrasts the hardware side with the software side, which involves culture and climate. The software side is more about creating the right atmosphere for innovation to develop. This includes having informal mechanisms that view creativity in a positive manner. This can include a culture based on a matrix organizational structure in which there is less of a hierarchy. This helps stimulate a more conducive innovation climate.

Sport organizations in a competitive environment can focus on innovation as a coping mechanism. This enables an organization to adapt strategically when they learn about potential sport innovation opportunities. In order to do this an organization may reposition themselves in the marketplace as both a sports club but also as a provider of other services. This repositioning strategy may involve some risk but if it is managed appropriately can have a better long-term outcome. Sometimes this means highlighting unmet or untapped needs that require market attention. For example, sports clubs can offer physiotherapy or sports nutrition services for sale that are based on the research and development undertaken within their organizations.

Strategic entrepreneurship

Strategic entrepreneurship involves focusing on opportunities that can be both explored and exploited in the marketplace (Kuratko, 2016). Part of the reason sports organizations focus on strategic entrepreneurship is to differentiate themselves from competitors while making fundamental changes. This enables new strategies to develop that provide better use of organizational capabilities. As part of the competitive nature of the sports industry it is important that organizations focus on strategies that help them succeed in the marketplace by focusing on potential profitability and market share.

Covin and Miles (1999) suggest that strategic entrepreneurship in organizations involves five forms: business model reconstruction, domain redefinition, organizational rejuvenation, strategic renewal and sustained rejuvenation. Business model reconstruction includes sports teams selling directly to fans rather than through intermediaries. The increased usage of electronic commerce has meant more sports teams can sell and communicate directly to consumers. Or alternatively business model changes might involve sports teams favoring corporate sponsors as a way to increase revenue rather than asking for donations. Domain redefinition includes a sports team moving into new directions such as other geographic markets. Organizational rejuvenation involves changing the way management is structured in order to instill a more innovative environment. This might include the use of new coaches or ways of thinking that challenge the current practices. Strategic renewal might include the building of a new stadium as a way to bring attention to a sport. Sustained regeneration involves continually looking for improvements in sport. This can take a broad range of activities from stadium reconstruction to improved services for fans at games.

Zahra (1991:259) describes corporate entrepreneurship as "those activities that enhance a company's ability to innovate, take risk, and seize opportunities in its markets." Corporate entrepreneurship occurs within an organization and can involve the business, division or project level (Zahra, 1991). There is normally a focus on internal activities within corporate entrepreneurship due to the risk of intellectual property or know how being misappropriated. Internal activities involve improving production methods, creation of new technologies or testing new administrative services. The innovations that originate from corporate entrepreneurship can occur in an informal manner, being unplanned activities. Although usually most sports innovations particularly the strategic ones develop from formal processes.

Little attention has been afforded to the role of corporate entrepreneurship in sport management. Missing from previous research is an effort to understand sport from a corporate entrepreneurship perspective. A corporate entrepreneurship approach to the study of sport provides for insight into the complexity of the process for sports innovation management. Essentially, corporate entrepreneurship attempts to examine the role of sport organizations in the development of business ventures that are influenced by innovation.

Koehler (1988:101) states "although sport organizations often take on a life and identity of their own, it should be never overlooked that the lifeline and energy of those organizations are lodged within individuals, especially the sport fitness managers." Sport managers have a variety of roles from coordinating, managing and administration in a sports organization (Koehler, 1988). Many sport managers are also involved in program development, marketing and facility management. These sport managers are part of the innovation process and help foster corporate entrepreneurship.

As for the interplay between sport and corporate entrepreneurship, there needs to be more concern about how organizational structure influences the dynamics of innovation. This may include looking into the involvement of sport managers in the decision-making processes that lead to corporate entrepreneurship. Some sport managers are better able to act strategically and create corporate ventures that have long-term viability.

There is still much needed to be revealed on how corporate entrepreneurship is enacted in sport settings. Many sport organizations decide to engage in corporate entrepreneurship in order to gain knowledge about innovation practices. To be successful the corporate entrepreneurship activity needs to be embedded within a sports organization's overall competitive strategies. The choice of using a corporate entrepreneurship strategy is a way sport organizations can use innovation on a sustained basis. Table 7.1 depicts the different stages of sport-based corporate entrepreneurship. These include sensing the change, galvanizing it and then enabling it to lead to radical alterations in the sport organization. At each stage of the change there are leadership, learning orientation, proactiveness and team orientation issues to take into consideration.

TABLE 7.1 Stages of sport-based corporate entrepreneurship

Type of stage	Stage 1	Stage 2	Stage 3
Level of change	Sensing change	Galvanizing change	Radical change
Leadership	Individuals	Managers and individuals	Whole organization
Learning orientation	Informal	Functional	Firm-wide initiatives
Proactiveness	Single champions	Information systems	Formal and informal processes
Team orientation	Linked	Top-down management approach	Lateral and vertical teams

Source: Adapted from Stopford and Baden-Fuller (1994).

Portfolio entrepreneurship

Sieger et al (2011:329) suggest there are many reasons for engaging in portfolio entrepreneurship and these include "growth aspirations, wealth and diversification, value maximization, and providing career opportunities for family members." Portfolio entrepreneurship is part of the sports landscape as many entrepreneurs and organizations in sport have multiple businesses. This occurs when two or more business opportunities are discovered, explored and grown (Wiklund and Shepherd, 2008). Portfolio entrepreneurship is when different levels of a sports organization are involved in a variety of ventures, including athletes establishing their own businesses, the team itself marketing products and services, and leadership becoming involved in public policy entrepreneurship.

The use of portfolio entrepreneurship as a theoretical lens to understand sports innovation is advocated because it enables a clear view of the innovation process. Portfolio entrepreneurship involves "an individual(s) simultaneously owning and engaging in a portfolio of entrepreneurial interests" (Carter and Ram, 2003:374). Chrisman et al (2003:442) state "entrepreneurship is a special case of strategic management." This is due to strategy involving the research for resources that need innovation to be created with portfolio entrepreneurship. Therefore, opportunities come from the renewal of interest in strategic objectives and do not just involve economic consideration but also rely on human desires to create value (Chrisman et al, 2003).

Central to understanding portfolio entrepreneurship is entrepreneurial intentions, which involve human behavior and its impact on entrepreneurship. Fini et al (2012:390) state "intentions evolve as individuals elaborate their knowledge, belief, attitudes and experiences." Thus, entrepreneurial intentions are important to sports organizations that rely on leadership to navigate new business ventures. These entrepreneurial intentions enable corporate ventures to form that utilize sports innovation. There are a variety of behavioral intention models based on theoretical frameworks existing in the literature. Depending on the discipline they might include social cognitive theory, which focuses on both internal and external environmental factors influencing behavioral intentions. Other behavioral intention models include the theory of reasoned action, which suggests individuals behave in certain ways depending on environmental stimuli. A more popular theory to explain behavioral intentions utilized in the entrepreneurship literature is the theory of planned behavior. This theory has its foundations in social psychology but has been adapted to suit the corporate entrepreneurship literature. The theory of planned behavior includes five main aspects "attitude toward behavior, subjective norms, perceived behavioral control, intention to behave and behavior" (Fini et al, 2012:390).

Innovation milieus

Stathopoulou et al (2004:406) state an innovation milieu is "an environment conducive to innovation." This means that sport has an innovation milieu as businesses can grow and prosper. As sport has local, regional and international elements, these different levels influence the innovation process in various ways. In the local environment there are socio-economic effects that mean corporate entrepreneurship develops as part of the communities' linkage to sport clubs. At the regional level the corporate entrepreneurship process is more complex as government and business entities work together on sports-related projects. At the international level, there is more of a dynamic process that effects the interaction of corporate entrepreneurship in sports.

The physical environment affects the development of corporate entrepreneurship in sport. Stathopoulou et al (2004:406) state "three major features of the physical environment highly effect entrepreneurship: location, natural resources and landscape." Location is important for sport as it influences the type of physical or electronic activity people engage in as part of their leisure time. Location involves the accessibility to customers, information sources, institutions, markets and suppliers (Stathopoulou et al, 2004). Some sports organizations are located close to major cities and this affects the type of businesses that are developed. Lower transportation costs between regions might influence sport organizations to produce products at cheaper rates than those in more distant regions. Although the internationalization of sport has meant that location is no longer a major issue as a result of new forms of technology making sport more easily accessible. In addition, the migration of sport fans to different locations has created opportunities for sport teams to develop new markets. This is reflected in the NFL playing games in Europe in order to capture more audiences in this geographic area. Alternatively, soccer clubs such as Manchester City have had a successful internationalization strategy by creating overseas partnership clubs like the one with Melbourne City in Australia.

Natural resources such as the sun, water and mountains have influenced the type of corporate entrepreneurship in sport. The development of the Santa Cruz skateboarding brand came from the city's beach location and skateboarding culture. The beach location allowed new businesses to be created in watersports, such as surfing, but also led to the development of connected sports, such as skateboarding. Thus, the landscape of a region in terms of being close to the beach has meant the development of related clothing and footwear businesses. Another example is the development of Havianas, the shoe company in Brazil, that originally sold shoes to workers as a cheap alternative to other footwear. Surfers then started wearing different colored Havianas and this created a fashion trend. This is also similar to Vans shoes, which were marketed as skateboarding shoes in Los Angeles, and then received broader market attention from other types of consumers. Hence, the location of a sport influences the associated businesses that develop as part of the linkage to the cultural element of the sport. Ugg boots are another example of a business developed from its association with a sport. Originally Ugg boots were worn by surfers after being in the water as they were warm and easy to put on. Ugg boots then became popular with non-surfers due to their warmth, fashion appeal and connection to the lifestyle of surfers.

Innovation in sport involves introducing new ideas that can be used to view things differently (Barrett and Sexton, 2006). This includes enhancing the standards and performance outcomes of sports organizations. In order to facilitate innovation there needs to be greater sensitivity to the practice of using new ideas in a positive manner. Innovation is a way organizations can be competitive but also is an end in itself. The development of innovation requires managerial skills that facilitate creating an appropriate environment to manage risk. This organizational climate includes focusing on matching personnel to roles that facilitate the integration of flexible decision-making processes. The market view of innovation suggests that the direction and quality of innovation is a result of market conditions (Barrett and Sexton, 2006). Spatial location is an important determinant of entrepreneurship and includes low-cost land, accessibility of transportation and proximity to educational institutions (Hurley, 1999).

In the sport industry there is a high level of social capital that supports networks of cooperation. This means that sports innovation is often considered a civic form of behavior as it has potential for the whole sport industry. The willingness of people in sport to trust each other facilitates innovative behavior that enables innovation. Therefore, a buildup of innovation results when there is networking and communication among people and businesses in sport.

Implications for sports managers

A better understanding of how to utilize corporate entrepreneurship in sport organizations is essential for sport managers. In both large and small sport organizations the creation of new businesses is helpful to overall performance. Greater attention should be paid by sport managers about how to strategically renew their organizations by focusing on corporate ventures. This may take the form of portfolio entrepreneurship that includes a set of related businesses ventures that are important to sports organizations. The development of entrepreneurial new ventures is important to managers as a revenue-enhancing strategy that can lead to better long-term performance.

Research on sport and corporate entrepreneurship is sparse and thus a deeper knowledge of the processes fostering it will be beneficial. The implementation of corporate entrepreneurship in sport will assist future development policies and enable the use of more effective policies to support corporate entrepreneurship. This chapter argues that the basis of corporate entrepreneurship processes in sport are not different to other industries but have unique characteristics. This is a result of sport having more government funding and non-profit entities involved in it than other industries. Sport imposes different constraints and opportunities that effect the development of corporate entrepreneurship in sport. This chapter places more emphasis on the concept of sport in the formation of corporate entrepreneurship.

Conclusion

This chapter has argued that an innovation perspective to sport business is important because of its linkage to corporate entrepreneurship. It reinforced the link between sport and business in terms of the psychology and types of activities. This chapter has attempted to make innovation a key component of sport business. Managers can enhance the power of sport by taking an innovation perspective. There will be a continued acceleration of innovation and much of the future sports innovations will be difficult to comprehend. This is due to new and emerging technology changing our current understanding about the role of sports innovation. Sports innovation possesses the crucial components needed to ensure success in organizations.

References

Barrett, P. and Sexton, M. (2006) 'Innovation in small, project-based construction firms', *British Journal of Management*, 17: 331–346.

Bruyat, C. and Julien, P.A. (2000) 'Defining the field of research on entrepreneurship', *Journal of Business Venturing*, 16: 165–180.

Carter, S. and Ram, M. (2003) 'Reassessing portfolio entrepreneurship', *Small Business Economics*, 21(4): 321–380.

Chrisman, J.J., Chua, J.H. and Steier, L.P. (2003) 'An introduction to theories of family business', *Journal of Business Venturing*, 18: 441–448.

Clark, J. (2009) 'Entrepreneurship and diversification on English farms: Identifying business enterprise characteristics and change processes', *Entrepreneurship & Regional Development*, 21(2): 213–236.

Covin, J.G. and Miles, M.P. (1999) 'Corporate entrepreneurship and the pursuit of competitive advantage', *Entrepreneurship Theory and Practice*, 23(3): 47–64.

Fini, R., Grimaldi, R., Marzocchi, G.L. and Sobrero, M. (2012) 'The determinants of corporate entrepreneurial intention within small and newly established firms', *Entrepreneurship Theory and Practice*, 36(2): 387–414.

Garner, J., Humphrey, P.R. and Simkins, B. (2016) 'The business of sport and the sport of business: A review of the compensation literature in finance and sports', *International Review of Financial Analysis*, 47: 197–204.

Gerrard, B. (2015) 'Rigour and relevance in sport management: Reconciling the competing demands of disciplinary research and user-value', *European Sport Management Quarterly*, 15(5): 505–515.

Hienerth, C. (2006) 'The commercialization of user innovations: The development of the rodeo kayaking industry', *R&D Management*, 36(3): 273–294.

Hornsby, J., Kuratko, D. and Zahra, S. (2002) 'Middle managers' perception of the internal environment for corporate entrepreneurship: Assessing a measurement scale', *Journal of Business Venturing*, 17(3): 253–273.

Hurley, A.G. (1999) 'Incorporating feminist theories into sociological theories of entrepreneurship', *Women in Management Review*, 14(2): 54–62.

Knoppers, A. (2015) 'Assessing the sociology of sport: On critical sport sociology and sport management', *International Review of the Sociology of Sport*, 50(4–5): 496–501.

Koehler, L.S. (1988) 'Job satisfaction and corporate fitness managers: An organizational behavior approach to sport management', *Journal of Sport Management*, 2: 100–105.

Kuratko, D.F. (2016) *Corporate Entrepreneurship: Accelerating Creativity and Innovation in Organisations*, Oxford University Press, Oxford.

Man, T.W.Y., Lau, T. and Chan, K.F. (2002) 'The competitiveness of small and medium enterprises: A conceptualization with focus on entrepreneurial competences', *Journal of Business Venturing*, 17: 123–142.

Roomi, M.A. and Harrison, P. (2010) 'Behind the veil: women-only entrepreneurship training in Pakistan', *International Journal of Gender and Entrepreneurship*, 2(2): 150–172.

Sahut, J.M. and Peris-Ortiz, M. (2014) 'Small business, innovation and entrepreneurship', *Small Business Economics*, 42: 663–668.

Shah, S. (2005) 'From innovation to firm formation in the windsurfing, skateboarding and snowboarding industries', Working paper No 05-0107, University of Illinois, Chicago, IL.

Sharma, P. and Chrisman, J.J. (1999) 'Toward a reconciliation of the definitional issues in the field of corporate entrepreneurship', *Entrepreneurship Theory and Practice*, 23(3): 11–28.

Shepherd, D.A. and Kuratko, D.K. (2009) 'The death of an innovative project: How grief recovery enhances learning', *Business Horizons*, 52(5): 451–458.

Sieger, P., Zellweger, T., Nason, R.S. and Clinton, E. (2011) 'Portfolio entrepreneurship in family firms: A resource-based perspective', *Strategic Entrepreneurship Journal*, 5: 327–351.

Smith, A. and Westerbeek, H. (2007) 'Sport as a vehicle for deploying corporate social responsibility', *Journal of Corporate Citizenship*, 25: 43–54.

Stathopoulou, S., Psaltopoulos, D. and Skuras, D. (2004) 'Rural entrepreneurship in Europe: A research framework and agenda', *International Journal of Entrepreneurial Behavior & Research*, 10(6): 404–425.

Stevenson, H. (1983) *A Perspective on Entrepreneurship*, Harvard Business School working paper, Cambridge, MA.

Stopford, J.M. and Baden-Fuller, C.W.F. (1994) 'Creating corporate entrepreneurship', *Strategic Management Journal*, 15: 521–536.

Thomas, S. and Potts, J. (2016) 'How industry competition ruined windsurfing', *Sport, Business and Management: An International Journal*, 6(5): 565–578.

Troilo, M. (2014) 'Adoption of technological innovation in a developing country: An empirical analysis of enterprises in Lao People's Democratic Republic', *Journal of Developmental Entrepreneurship*, 19(3): 1–15.

Wiklund, J. and Shepherd, D.A. (2008) 'Portfolio entrepreneurship: Habitual and novice founders, new entry, and mode of organizing', *Entrepreneurship Theory and Practice*, 32(4): 701–725.

Zahra, S. (1991) 'Predictors and financial outcomes of corporate entrepreneurship: An exploratory study', *Journal of Business Venturing*, 6: 259–285.

8
TECHNOLOGY INNOVATION

Introduction

This chapter investigates technological innovation in sport. By building on technology innovation research, the chapter discusses that more emphasis in sport needs to be placed on the role of technology for innovation. This helps to gain a deeper understanding about the ability of technology innovation to create value in sport organizations. As technology is changing sport, there needs to be greater attention placed on its role in innovation.

The purpose of this chapter is to offer a view of sports innovation by focusing on technology. This allows an exploration about how emerging technologies are changing the way sport is viewed and practiced. More specifically, the aim of this chapter is to outline a technology innovation view of sport and the relevant theoretical framework to understand innovation in sport. Whereas mainstream technology innovation has received considerable attention in research, less is analyzed at the sport level. Introducing a technology innovation perspective in sport is timely due to the rapid emergence of computers and information systems changing sport management. This chapter seeks to answer the following main questions. First, how is technological innovation changing sport management? And second, what kind of technology is having the biggest impact on sports innovation?

This chapter makes three main contributions to the sport, innovation and technology literature. First, the concept of sport technology innovation is elaborated upon and refined. Second, the role of technology in sport innovation is explained to justify focusing more on technology in sports management research. This helps to build an understanding of how technology is shaping and influencing the sports industry. Third, the impact of sports technology on society is explained in order to capture the changing attitudes toward technology in sport.

This chapter is structured as follows. The role of technology innovation is examined that leads to a focus on sports. Next, different ways of analyzing technology innovation in sport are stated. Then, suggestions for future technology innovations and forecasting demand in sport are stated. Working on the intersection of sport and technology innovation scholarship, this chapter will move sport management research into an emerging interdisciplinary field. In doing so this chapter reveals how the technological innovations in sport impact performance. Ultimately, this chapter encourages people to see the value of expanding sports management into the technology literature. Currently, there is little explicit link between sports innovation and technology management so this chapter provides a good overview of the linkages.

Process of innovation

Barrett and Sexton (2006:342) state, "the process of innovation is behavioural in nature, being a cyclical process of diagnosing, action planning, taking action, evaluating and specifying learning." This means for technological innovation to occur there needs to be a link to how it can improve sports performance. Part of this process will involve diagnosing what the technology will do in sport and then planning actions to implement it properly. Some technologies may take money and time to develop so there needs to be an evaluation process in terms of costs and benefits. Once this is complete individuals and organizations can learn about how to use the sports technology.

The managers of sports organizations have the power to ensure that innovation activity around sport takes place. The triggers for technology innovation are generally filtered by sports managers in terms of their likelihood of having an impact on their organizations. This means prioritizing the most important technology innovations through a process of systemic thinking. This will involve coming up with a vision for the technology innovation and how it can be progressed.

The goal for most sport technology innovations is to close the gap between the current and future desired level of performance. This can mean for every advancement in technology there may be a step backwards in terms of opportunity costs in the form of time and money before it advances in the marketplace. Hence, there is action and reaction in sports technology innovation that is part of the evolutionary process, which is stated in Table 8.1.

TABLE 8.1 Action and reaction in sports technology innovation

Type of activity	Examples
Action	Leadership and management support
	Allocation of resources and time
Reaction	Resistance to change from organizational members and stakeholders
	Lack of coordination for the innovation
	Inability to access staff to channel innovation

Source: Adapted from Sexton and Barrett (2003).

Innovation and sport

Sport-based forms of organizations are inadequately addressed in the technology innovation literature. The sports industry's emphasis on technology has the potential to provide useful insights for innovation efforts in other types of industries. The sport industry is generally driven by social and profit-orientated projects that have a complex array of stakeholders involved in their growth. However, innovation is sometimes hard to predict due to the interaction and feedback needed for its advancement in the market. This is especially evident in uncertain environments that provide unknown market conditions. This has resulted in the management of innovation being referred to as controlled chaos due to its uncertain nature (Quinn, 1985). There is often a significant difference in the ability of small organizations to innovate due to resource constraints and lack of capacity. This may provide a trigger for large organizations to focus on technology innovation as a way to increase their market share. However, large organizations can be less agile and have a bureaucratic structure that slows the pace of innovation (Floyd and Lane, 2000).

Sport unites people as it transcends language and cultural barriers. Often sport is used to capture innovation as it combines different types of activities. Sport is increasing in popularity especially as more people emphasize leisure activities and their health. This is in conjunction with the globalization of sport made possible by technology innovations such as the internet. Innovation is central to sport management research. Sport is complex as there are a variety of different activities included within this field. This helps to link sport to technology innovation in order to progress our understanding about sport.

There is a romantic attraction to sport due to the emotional effect it has on people's lives. This means that sport is embedded in communities and technology is often viewed both as an advantage and disadvantage depending on its use. Some technology such as online statistics of players and teams are viewed as a useful addition to the sports field. Other technology including new stadiums that take away from the historical background of a sport may be viewed as a disadvantage.

There is surprisingly little research about sports technology innovation despite its prominence in practical settings. This is unfortunate given there is so much to learn about the way sport integrates technology innovation. There is potential conflict between integrating sport and technology innovation. This is due to sport having historical significance in society that may be changed by the use of technology innovation. There is a need for the use of technology innovation by sport communities in their delivery of services. The technology can bridge the relationships between community, government and sporting organizations. There is much work to be done in measuring how technology contributes to sport and ways to nurture technological innovations. This can help attract more diverse forms of technology innovations to sport.

Much has been written about the influence of technology in sport as a result of the rapidly changing innovations being introduced into the marketplace. Technology is the essence of much of sport innovation in business. In the current competitive environment, the ability to integrate technology innovation into sport may be the most relevant factor influencing performance. This is because innovation is a behavior that needs to be incorporated more into a sports context.

Intrapreneurship

Intrapreneurship is when entrepreneurship occurs within an established organization and is the means by which new ideas, philosophies and products are identified (Rule and Irwin, 1988). Many sports managers believe intrapreneurship is a way of including technology innovation into their organizations. The inclusion of technology innovations is a strategic priority for many sport organizations but there are different ways technology innovation can contribute to sports organizations. This includes new research and development into better playing techniques using data analytics. It can also involve transferring new ideas to sports organizations using technology.

Technology is playing a crucial role in the development of sports-related products and services. The rate of sports technology development is astounding as it has changed the way we view sport. Innovation involves the use of networks in order to access and disseminate ideas to bring about change. Often these networks in sport involve cooperating with partners who have a different motive or reason for innovation. Interpersonal relationships facilitate the networked innovation process as they enable both verbal and non-verbal communication (D'Antone et al, 2017).

Sports innovation is shaped by business networks and societal interactions, which determine the ease and rate of change. There is continuous evolution of sports innovations as they are integrated into the market. D'Antone et al (2017:1) state "the emergence and construction of innovation in markets is a result of interactions not only between organizations, but also between human and non-human elements." This has meant that sports innovation often takes place through broad social-technical transformation that goes beyond business networks as they include societal effects (D'Antone et al, 2017). Market innovation includes exchange, representation and normalizing. In sport, the exchange includes all the related activities that are needed to progress the change. This representation means focusing on current sports conditions to see how they can innovate. Normalizing involves trying to make the sport change occur in a real sense.

Corporate innovation communication is defined as "a group of individuals, consisting of both employees and external innovators, who work on a voluntary basis on innovative activities for a certain company." Members of these communities can work in a physical or online environment to develop innovations. Sport has experienced pressure to change from reduced government funding and the need to find alternative revenue. There has been an increase in the level of user innovation in sport. This has resulted from the use of more technology in the form of online communication in sport.

Sports organizations need to be innovative in order to survive. The notion of innovation in sport has been widely discussed in the media but less in a research context. There is currently a gap between the sport management and innovation literature in linking both fields of study to come up with an explanation of sports innovation. Innovation might be relevant in particular settings but unimportant in certain sports contexts. This has led to a lack of corroboration about sports innovation management.

In sport, there is a constant flow of innovation but it is unclear how the innovation occurred. This has prompted more interest in studying the environmental contexts around sport to understand the process. There are often unique intricacies of innovation in sport that require a more dynamic understanding. The sports innovation process involves the interactions and reactions between different entities. Sometimes this requires sports entities to act in a way that enables greater use of the environmental context. The sports environment is complex and needs to be analyzed in a holistic manner.

In a study of innovation in an amateur sports organization Caza (2000) refers to the importance of receptive and non-receptiveness in the change process. Receptive context is defined as "features of context (and management action) that seem to be favourably associated with forward movement" (Pettigrew et al, 1992:98). In some sports contexts such as the clothing industry there is a receptive context due to the need to keep up-to-date with fashion but also new types of fabric. In other sports contexts that have a more traditional outlook there is less receptivity to change as they prefer to keep the status quo. This is seen with older sports such as tennis keeping the same rules despite advances in scoring technology. Non-receptive contexts are defined as "a configuration of features that may be associated with blocks on change" (Pettigrew et al, 1992:208). Often this occurs in highly regulated sports such as football that require key institutional support to bring about change. In sports such as swimming there was a reluctance to use new swimsuits due to the effects they had on performance.

There needs to be a clarity of goals in the production of a sports innovation. This helps make the outcomes from the sports innovation clearly understood. As a result of increased technological advances the timing of a sports innovation may be a strategic weapon. This means that during the sports innovation process there needs to be a focus on the reasons for the change in order to limit the distractions. Sometimes being a first mover in a sports innovation will be important to build momentum and bring about brand recognition. This is evident with sports camera technology such as GoPro being a leader as a result of their early entry into the market.

There is no authoritative definition of sports innovation, which means there is diversity in meanings. Many sports innovations are preemptive actions that are taken to increase enjoyment or performance. This can include new administrative systems in a sport that facilitate better viewing experiences. For example, the increased ability of sports media to focus on different elements of a game have led to more flexibility in viewing experiences. Sports innovation is not a discrete act but rather involves a number of steps that are improved based on feedback.

Sports organizations need to innovate to capitalize on opportunities that give them a competitive edge. Changing technologies mean there is a need for sports organizations to value add to their existing portfolios. In sport, the term innovation can reflect a wide range of changes from operations, people, products and services. The sports innovation literature is more recent than mainstream innovation literature due to the increased amount of time and money spent on leisure activities in society. The implementation of new behaviors in sport is part of the innovation process. The adoption of innovative behaviors is a way for sports organizations to maintain a competitive edge. This helps to generate new ideas that lead to market improvements.

Seifried et al (2016:2) state "there remains a surprising dearth of research of the intersection of diffusion and sport." The diffusion is the way innovation is spread and understood within a set context. Thus, innovation diffusion involves adopting an innovation within a social system and communicating it to other members of a community (Rogers, 2003). Sometimes innovation takes time to be understood in a social system so it helps when more people can relate to the relevance of the sports innovation. The diffusion of innovation can be analyzed by focusing on the way and how it spreads (Kimberly and Evanisko, 1981).

There are some barriers to the diffusion of innovation including communication systems, geography and time (Seifried et al, 2016). Social systems can help with the diffusion process by encouraging the neighborhood effect to take place (Lanzolla and Suarez, 2012). The neighborhood effect means that there is likely to be more adoption of innovations when people and organizations are geographically close to each other. This physical proximity or more increasingly an online connection can encourage the sports innovation to spread to other people or organizations. This is a form of knowledge spillover as the information about the sports innovation is discussed among a group of people.

Sports teams and athletes have a neighborhood effect as they often use the same playing fields or share use of certain products that helps to transfer knowledge. Once an athlete or team adopts a sports innovation there is likely to be a bandwagon effect to others. Some sports organizations have tried to market their innovations by branding them with logos. This helps create an innovation community as the actions and thoughts are communicated to others. As sport is watched through the television and internet by a global community the sports innovations can have a rapid uptake if marketed in the right way.

The timing of sports innovation into the market is important to its success. In sports innovations that might be user-driven or protected by intellectual property, this impacts the time needed for an innovation to be developed then adopted by consumers. Some sports innovations might need testing in the market, which is why athlete or team endorsements are important. This endorsement helps others to understand the usefulness of an innovation.

Innovation decision processes

Rogers (2003) suggest that there are five stages of the innovation decision process: knowledge, persuasion, decision, implementation and confirmation. Sports innovations that are less risky, such as those that are product-based, are likely to go through these stages more quickly than sports medicine that requires regulatory approval. The first stage of knowledge means people becoming aware of the newness and how it can influence their behavior. Knowledge can come from a variety of sources including athletes, coaches, fans, government and organizations. The knowledge can be tacit in terms of sports experience or explicit in terms of codified material.

The second stage of persuasion involves gathering information about the sports innovations' cost and effectiveness in the market. Some sports innovations such as new technology devices may be developed in collaboration with non-sports entities as they have impact outside of sports. This means that the persuasion will focus on the perceived characteristics of the innovation, which are relative advantage, compatibility, complexity, trialability and observability (Seifried et al, 2016). The relative advantage of a sports innovation means looking at what is currently done and how it can be improved.

Seifried et al (2016:14) state "while the sports industry continues to change, current managers in the sporting industry can continue to learn by looking backwards to their history rather than merely forwards to the future." The past is helpful sometimes in predicting the nature and flow of sports innovations. Most of the previous sports innovations involved products that impacted the way games were played. In addition, there were social innovations in terms of encouraging diversity in terms of race, age and sex in sport but more needs to be done in terms of this equality. Despite college sports in the United States having legislation ensuring there is equal funding to male and female sports, there still is a lack of media attention on female sports players and females in general in the sports industry. Hence, sports innovation needs to further utilize social change as a way to bridge the gap between equality and diversity initiatives. Compatibility of sports innovation with current products, services and technologies is important to ensuring its adoption. As some sports organizations or people spend money on an existing innovation, leveraging future ideas based on the first mover in the industry is important. Complexity involves how detailed or useful a sports innovation is in terms of its application. Some sports innovations, such as the use of new media, require vast amounts of money spent on their research and development. This means that sports media innovations might be expensive but offer a lot of services. Trialability involves using the sports innovation in a practical sense to see how people like it and whether it is worth purchasing. Some sports organizations will trial an innovation such as a new clothing fabric in wet and dry conditions to assess its suitability on the field. Observability means seeing how others are using a sports innovation to assess its likely useability for them. This can occur in other industries then be applied to the sports field.

The third stage is about the decision, which involves adopting or rejecting the sports innovation. The adoption can be time dependent with some users being early adopters and others late, depending on their attitude toward the innovation. As part of the adoption some users of the sports innovation may decide it does not work for them and reject it but others may show their friends and this has a contagion effect. As sports teams and athletes are known by their community it helps with the adoption process if the innovation is shared within their social network.

The fourth stage implementation involves integrating the change to suit the environmental context. This may mean that all teams or athletes adopt the innovation. The fifth stage of confirmation involves users deciding whether the sports innovation is good or bad. This can mean the future viability and commercialization of the sports innovation is dependent on the opinion of the users.

Inclusive innovation

The benefits from a sports innovation are not always automatic as it may involve inequalities or costs. This has meant the term "inclusive innovation" has become popular as a way of assessing the benefits of an innovation to a society. Inclusive innovation involves the inclusion of groups who are marginalized within the innovation. In sport for development, inclusive innovation is a way to encourage people in less-developed countries to participate in sport. Moreover, inclusive innovation in sport may involve the creation of business models to make sport more affordable.

Cooke (2016:1496) states innovation "is a recombination of knowledge and artefacts that consist largely of already existing entities." Sports innovations can range from completely new ideas to the addition of features within existing products to improve them. This means that some sports innovations may be familiar as they have been developed in other industries then applied to sport. For example, the use of organic cotton in sportswear that was originally developed for general clothing usage but has an extra benefit in sports as it is advertised as sustainable and cooling when worn. This means that sports innovation needs to have a commercial or practical sense so it can be applied in the market.

Sports innovation in organizations often involves a group of people working together. This can include the inventor or person who comes up with the idea for the sports innovation. Some ideas happen by serendipity as a result of playing sport or being involved in the sports industry. Once an idea has evolved it normally needs an entrepreneur who realizes the potential of the sports innovation. This means thinking of the idea in terms of commercializing it and making it accessible for a fee. This commercialization involves a process from financing the innovation to marketing it to retail outlets. Some of this financial aspect to sports innovation is risky as there may be a degree of uncertainty about the likelihood of success. Last, there needs to be a sports innovation manager who strategizes about the sports innovation and makes key decisions.

Knowledge flows

There is growing recognition in understanding the influence of innovation in the context of sport. In particular, analyzing the knowledge flows to sports innovation is important. Explicit knowledge involves "information that can be easily communicated and acted upon among individuals" (Huggins and Prokop, 2016:4). Tacit knowledge "such as skills, competences and talents—is more difficult to directly communicate to someone else in a verbal or other symbolic form" (Huggins and Prokop, 2016:4). There are two main modes to utilize knowledge for innovation (Jensen et al, 2007). These modes can work together in helping knowledge about potential sport innovations become a reality. The first mode involves the use of science and technology within innovations. In sport, there are continued advances in technology and medicine affecting the development of innovations. Sports science can include the use of new medicine to improve sports performance. This has been a controversial area due to the potential harm done to athletes by the use of some new substances. This has created a dilemma as some sport science innovations can be beyond the current ethical practices. Technology also creates a dilemma in terms of how the innovation changes the way sport currently functions. The second mode involves doing, interacting and using (Huggins and Prokop, 2016). This is important in sport as innovations need to be carried out in a practical setting to ensure people use them. This can involve learning by experience about what types of sport innovations will work in practice. By involving others in the process this helps to refine the sports innovation.

Regional innovation systems

Regional innovation systems are a way of facilitating inventions and ideas around sport. Asheim and Coenen (2005:1177) define regional innovation systems as "the institutional infrastructure supporting innovation within the production structure of a region." Regions are important to sports innovation as they facilitate knowledge transfer, which is important in cities such as New York that are known for their high-profile sports teams. In addition, often governments will promote sport-based regional innovation systems as a way to encourage business and people to relocate to a certain region. This is seen in Melbourne, Australia hosting premier sports events such as the Australian Tennis Open, which is the only grand slam event in the Asia-Pacific region. This has resulted in Melbourne becoming a sports precinct known for hosting international events that have encouraged further investment in sport. Thus, sports innovation policy is often based on the region or geographic area.

Brown et al (2016:1262) state that in regional innovation systems "universities, public sector research organizations, skills development bodies, regulatory bodies and increasingly venture capitalists are key actors." Therefore, universities often focus on sport as a way to encourage community engagement but also bring financial rewards to a region. This is often seen in college towns in the United States such as Syracuse being known for its sports teams.

Innovation systems occur at the regional, national and sectoral level, which are all important in the development of sports innovation. This is a result of government policy playing an important role in shaping sports innovation through entrepreneurial contexts. Innovation is often relationally embedded in a region and this influences the type of new sports products and services developed. As creativity plays an important role in sports innovation it helps to focus on how government policies can be coordinated within the innovation process. In sport, the government policies can help to bridge the different actors and entities that facilitate sports innovation.

Sports compete for investment as a way of promoting their quality and distinctiveness. Governments are often a source of funding for sports as they encourage the growth of public resources such as parks and recreation facilities that sports teams utilize. There is potential value in developing sports innovation as a source of growth and employment. This has international relevance as sport provides a context for innovations to develop. Sports innovation has significant geographic reach and relevance as a result of its international popularity.

Sport entities that ignore potential innovations will be left behind. Sports innovation has become a significant way that organizations derive revenue and increase their global competitiveness. Sport organizations can achieve an innovative output that enables them to compete with leaders in other industries. Sport and innovation are interconnected due to the increasing importance of knowledge as a source of competitiveness. In some sports contexts there is inadequate infrastructure and a lack of openness that holds organizations back from innovating. For example, the less-resourced sports such as lawn bowls that have fallen in popularity have poorer levels of innovation. Sports innovation underpins the emergence of sport as a global phenomenon enjoyed by many people.

There are a variety of inter-organizational relationships required in sport including governments, organizations, media, community, sponsors, volunteers, employees and fans. Parent et al (2016:1) state that in sport the stakeholder network "is a multi-sectorial network with non-profit, for-profit and public organizations." Stakeholder networks and inter-organizational relationships are endemic in sport and needed for innovation. Networks exist in a set of relationships that are dependent on a context. The complexities of a network mean that there needs to be social coordination in order to ensure connectivity. Networks in a sport context involve different environments such as digital, workplace and leisure, which influence the types of exchanges that take place.

Sport, due to its emphasis on non-profit and community involvement as well as its profit role, has a pervasive set of networks. They are based on the exchange of information and are often needed for sport to function properly. For sports innovation to progress there needs to be benefits to a network that enable opportunities to occur. This might mean the connections between people in a network are dependent on the level of discussion that leads to innovation. Some sports networks are more formalized and structured, such as team events, but others are less regulated and occur in an informal manner based on mutual interests. Some sports teams, such as Manchester City Football Club, have a large international network due to the diaspora of fans living in multiple locations. Thus, some sports networks will be denser in concentration based on the emotional attachment people feel to a certain sport or team. Some sports networks are highly centralized and this affects the authoritative role in terms of access and dissemination of information. Other sport networks act as information hubs that facilitate shared interests about a sport.

Sport has utilized regional innovation systems to create new teams based on population density. This is a form of sports innovation as the new teams typically go into locations that are lacking in access to a sport as a way to develop more interest in the game. This is evident in new teams being started in strategic geographic locations such as "New York City Football Club in America, Western Sydney Wanderers in Australia and Ottawa Redblacks in Canada" (McDonald et al, 2016:136).

Sports innovation culture

There have been traditionally disciplinary boundaries between sport and innovation that became entrenched as a result of specialized associations and journals. This disciplinary divide is more in theory rather than practice as there are blurred boundaries between sport and innovation due to their similar competitive natures. More recently there has been increased advocacy for interdisciplinary studies that merge different areas of study (Anggadwita et al, 2017). This has led to increased scholarly interest in sports innovation as it cross-pollinates two distinct topic areas of sport and innovation. The historical divergence and separation between sport and innovation was a result of sport being seen as more of a physical science and kinesiology subject with less emphasis on business. This has changed with the emergence of sport management studies linking the intersection of sport and business. The recent intellectual emphasis on sports business has enabled the disciplines of sport and innovation management to be studied more closely.

The key to initiating sports innovation lies within the stakeholder members of a sport and the degree to which the spirit of innovation can be initiated. Sport often flourishes when innovation is introduced as captured as part of the sport's progress in society. Innovation in sport requires people to listen and respond to change. The hope of many in sport is that it becomes more innovative as a way to progress. Often the culture within a sport will need to foster the innovation to ensure its success. For sports innovation to flourish, more needs to be known about the process of innovation and how it can be progressed. The explanation of sports innovation needs to be understood as a collection of different entities based on the ability of sport to act innovatively. A sports innovator has the profile of being a risk manager and networker.

Culture is evident within a sports context and includes "within different levels (national, regional, business, individual), layers of society (gender, age, social, class, occupation, family, religion) and in varying contexts of life (individual, group, community)" (Morrison, 2000:60). In sport there are national, regional and international institutions that regulate conduct in the industry and need to adopt innovations in order for them to be successful. This is seen in some sports having their games innovated based on changing styles of play and behavior. This is evident in surfing, with rules such as having priority, meaning that each surfer takes in turn surfing a wave. In addition, in surfing there has been the introduction of technology in the form of jet skis to help surfers reach waves faster than paddling out themselves. There has also been an increase in big wave surfing with surfers wearing inflatable wetsuits as a form of flotation device when needed.

At the individual level athletes have been innovative with their use of clothing and symbols. An example is Usain Bolt, the multiple Olympic champion sprinter, who makes the lightning bolt symbol with his arms after every race. This symbol is trademarked by Usain Bolt as a way of differentiating himself and adding a bit of entertainment to the sports market. At the business level are the apparel and equipment that go with a sport. For example, the National Basketball Association licenses certain sportswear makers to produce clothing.

In terms of society, there are demographics that influence sports innovation. These include gender-based sports having more women or men such as cheerleading for women and football for men. However, there has been more gender equality in these sports in recent years. Age is another characteristic that has influenced sports innovations particularly around slower leisure activities such as walking. Despite the age restrictions in playing some professional sports there have been older athletes playing competitively for longer time periods.

Case study: Kelly Slater and surfing innovation

Kelly Slater is an American professional surfer who has become the most successful and enduring athlete on the World Professional Surfing Tour. He has won a total of 11 World Surfing titles and is the youngest (at 21 years old) and oldest (at 39 years old) to win a World Surfing title. He is considered one of the most influential surfers in history with his ability to connect surfing to a worldwide global audience and his promotion of surfing as a sport. He is a global sports brand that has evolved to become one of the most appealing and lucrative surfers on the surfing scene. The timeline below indicates the important innovations Kelly Slater has been involved with in terms of surfing and sport.

Timeline of events

1972 Kelly Slater born in Cocoa Beach, Florida
1980 Enters first surfing competition at 8 years old

1990 Begins being sponsored by Quiksilver after a bidding war with other surfing brands takes place
1991 Becomes a professional surfer and enters into the World Surfing Professional Association World Tour
1992 Becomes the youngest World Surfing Champion; Appears on four episodes of Baywatch
1994–1998 Wins five consecutive World Surfing Championships
1997 Becomes most successful all-time record holder of World Surfing Championships
1998 Releases album "Songs from the Pipe"
2003–2004 Competes in X Games
2003 Publishes autobiography *Pipe Dreams: A Surfer's Journey*
2005 In final heat of Billabong Tahiti Pro at Teahupolo becomes first surfer to be awarded two perfect scores for a total of 20 out of 20 points
2007 Passes fellow American Tom Curren's World Tour victory of 33 championships
2010 United States House of Representatives honors him for his surfing achievements
2011 Becomes the oldest World Surfing Champion
2013 Wins Quiksilver Pro at Gold Coast, Australia at 41 years of age and ranked number one on the World Surfing Tour

Impact on development of surfing as a professional sport

Kelly Slater is one of the most dominant athletes in history who, for the past two decades, has continued to redefine surfing by promoting it as a professional sport. Kelly was originally an amateur surfing champion who won six Eastern Surfing Association Titles and four National Titles before he became a professional surfer in 1990. During his early years on the World Surfing Tour, Kelly changed existing surfing styles by introducing the "new school" of surfing. This new school consisted of more radical wave moves that incorporated a greater level of athleticism that was previously not evident in the sport. As Kelly incorporated more innovative wave movements his celebrity brand was being established by his television and magazine appearances. At 19 years old he was named by *People Magazine* as one of the world's "50 most beautiful people," and this created a more widespread visibility in professional surfing that encouraged a lifestyle approach to the sport. As he won more World Surfing titles, his high-profile relationships with actresses and models such as Pamela Anderson, Gisele Bündchen and Cameron Diaz kept him in the celebrity pages as a well-known sports star. This led to him becoming a global brand with a strong international recognition that encouraged more people to try surfing as a sport and also follow the World Championship Tour events around the world. In addition, he was among the first surfers to design his own video game (Kelly Slater Pro-Surfer), which broadened his appeal. His appearances on numerous surfing videos such as the recent 3D Imax Film "The Ultimate Wave Tahiti" increased his online presence brand as a revolutionary surfer and professional athlete.

As part of his influence on the future direction of professional surfing he has instigated a number of changes to the rules and regulations of surfing competitions. These include the introduction of shorter time periods in the competitive schedule and the introduction of the priority system. The priority system enables faster surfing periods in which surfers in a competition must give preference on a wave to the surfer who was not the previous rider of a wave instead of competing on the same wave in the water. These innovations also led to an attempt in 2009 to launch his own professional surfing circuit called "The Rebel Tour." However, this was stopped by the Association of Surfing Professionals. His leadership as a global surfing ambassador has helped push surfing into mainstream sports. Part of this ambassador role has been his involvement with ESPN and the X-Games to bring sport in line with other adventure and action sports including skiing and BMX racing. This relationship as evident in 2013 when ESPN named Kelly Slater as the most influential figure in action sports for his role in shaping the future development of surfing.

Quiksilver partnership

For most of Kelly Slater's career he has been sponsored by Quiksilver. Quiksilver was originally started in the 1960s in Torquay, Australia as a surfing brand that has since become one of the most popular surfing brands around the world. Quiksilver originally sponsored Kelly because of his future surfing potential but also for his linkages to the American surfing market and his international appeal. Kelly Slater's sponsorship from Quiksilver has meant that he wears its clothing line but also owns 3 percent of the company in stock. This stock ownership is worth approximately $22 million and cements the relationship between Kelly Slater and Quiksilver for his remaining professional surfing career. The connection between Kelly Slater and Quiksilver has been mutually beneficial for both as Quiksilver has grown more than 1000 percent since the first signing of Kelly Slater as a major surfing star and now is a dominant surfing brand in the North American market. In addition, he owns a Quiksilver Los Angeles store that showcases some of his trophies from his surfing career. The popularity of Quiksilver's sponsorship of Kelly Slater led to the 2012 introduction of a new Kelly Slater clothing line that focused on casual adventure apparel that has an environmental component in the use of organic and sustainable fabric.

Technology's role in surfing development

Kelly Slater has facilitated the increased usage of technology in surfing that coincided with the introduction of the internet and multimedia technology to consumers. The introduction of live streaming of surfing events has revolutionized the way people view surfing as increasing numbers of new innovations, such as the radio-automated cameras flying over surf events, has changed viewing capabilities. In 2013, Kelly Slater tied in more of his business ventures to technology by launching a new website KSwaveco.com that designs wave pools. This website is based on his Kelly Slater Wave Company philosophy of bridging the gaps between surf, lifestyle and technology. His company has become an industry leader in wave science by taking an innovative approach to wave generation and control technology. He has become one of the first professional surfers to link his surfing achievements to the development of a company which designs surf experiences in a controlled environment, guaranteeing waves and entertainment. His company has applied for a number of wave technology patents and has been in talks to develop wave parks around the world.

Kelly Slater Foundation and philanthropic endeavors

Kelly Slater's major achievements include broadening the exposure of surfing and enhancing the marketability of surfing by bringing the sport of surfing to a wider global audience. He is one of the most prolific athletes of all time and has had a major influence on modern surfing. The Kelly Slater brand has become known for his professionalism and philanthropic character, and this is used as a consistent and trusted marketing tool. The Kelly Slater Foundation is a registered not-for-profit located in Los Angeles, California. It was founded in 2007 to raise awareness for existing social and environmentally conscious charities. The purpose of the foundation is to host specialty fundraising events by collaborating with organizations and philanthropists to support charitable causes. Some of the events the foundation has hosted are the Kelly Slater International, which is a surf, music and lifestyle event. There is also a donation program called Kelly's 10's for Kids Program that goes to a pre-school program enabling special needs children to learn among their peers.

The final score

Kelly Slater has dominated professional surfing during the past 20 years. He is considered the most successful professional athlete and his achievements are superior to many other professional athletes in sports such as basketball and football. His net worth is estimated to be over US$22 million, which includes winning the most prize money (more than US$3 million) and becoming the first "seven-figure" salary surfer. No other athlete currently surpasses Kelly Slater's dominance of professional surfing or his longevity in a sport that is physically demanding. He has won the most events of any surfer with 52 World Surfing titles and is considered one of the most successful surfers of all time.

Sport and social issues

Social class equality involves people from different income levels playing sport and, despite change, this largely still applies to sports such as golf. There are more professional than amateur athletes now due to the money paid to sports people.

In the past, athletes often had to have another career while pursuing sports, but this is now changing with more professional athletes in sport. Family is part of sport and this is evident in many coaching arrangements, such as those with tennis players like Rafael Nadal who is coached by his uncle. Religion is part of sport but this is often not talked about due to its sensitive nature. Changes in societal attitudes have meant the sports games are now played on religious holidays. For example, Australian Football league games are now played on Good Friday, which was traditionally a non-playing time.

The introduction of sports innovation can occur at different levels of life, such as the individual, with more people focusing on new adventure sports such as kitesurfing, which is typically done by one person but often in a group. This has given rise to communities of like-minded sports enthusiasts joining together to innovate their sport. Sports culture involves a set of learned behaviors that are part of the conduct in a certain sport. Some sports have a culture based on certain attitudes that are reflected in ways things are done. This influences the way members of a sports community share ideas and contribute to innovation.

Some of the sports culture is institutionalized from regulatory authorities deeming certain behaviors acceptable. Other sports cultures have evolved to include societal expectations about appropriate behavior. There is also a political aspect to some sports cultures as there are entrenched behaviors that are hard to change. For example, there are few female football umpires or professional players despite societal pushes toward gender equity. Table 8.2 depicts the sport culture by providing examples of personal characteristics, societal influencers and behaviors.

Sports organizations that have knowledge about innovations are capable of creating successful new products and services. Both product usefulness and originality are important in the development of sports innovations. Newness is a key concept in innovation and applies to sport as it is important for competitiveness. Sports innovation is a means to create a competitive advantage, which is important given the quickly changing technological advancements being made in society. New opportunities in sport help increase advancements in technology and related industries. There are more frequent shifts in consumer demand for sports products, which is fueling innovation.

TABLE 8.2 Sport culture

Personal characteristics	*Societal influencers*	*Behaviors*
Culture	Classes	Aspirations
Education	Contexts	Attitudes
Family	Economics	Attributes
History	Institutions	Hopes
Religion	Policy	Ideologies
	Structures	Values

Source: Adapted from Morrison (2000).

The increased stream of knowledge keeps sport organizations in perpetual change and affects innovation rates. Sports organizations need to focus more on being innovative in order to sustain their market appeal. Innovation is more than change as it needs to go beyond alterations to introduce originality into the market (Tsiotsou and Ratten, 2010). This means a feature of innovation is novelty as it enables the exploitation of change.

Johannessen et al (2001:22) state innovation includes "any policy, structure, method or process, or any product or market opportunity that the manager of an innovating unit perceives to be new." Thus, innovation involves ideas or practices that are perceived to be new. The economic performance of sports organizations requires that there is a progressive introduction of new ideas. This means that innovation in sport can be a vague concept and needs to be clarified before being understood.

There are external and internal influences of sports innovation that can predict likely success. External influences include customer-supplier relations, market conditions and knowledge infrastructures (Johannessen et al, 2001). In sport, these external influences often need to work together to co-create the innovation. In order to stimulate innovation there needs to be networks between the external partners. This provides a source for encouraging sports innovation and emphasizes the collaboration required for innovation. Some networks may have stronger ties due to the historical or personal nature of their association (Tajeddini and Ratten, 2017). Internal factors include culture, communication and learning processes (Johannessen et al, 2001). By focusing on newness, these internal factors can link organization structure to facilitate the innovation process. Sports innovation differs from imitation as it requires original thought and action. To encourage newness organizations need to have new organizing personnel and skills (Johannessen et al, 2001). This helps to promote management systems that can evolve to produce innovation.

Innovation and sports management

Barneva and Hite (2017:326) state sport management is "an interdisciplinary branch of learning between physical education, business, psychology, history, law and communications." Sport management emphasizes the practical nature of physical sciences and fitness within a business setting. Innovation in sport can occur in a range of settings including business operations, event management and facility management. In addition, there is innovation in marketing and communications, ticketing and sales, and recruitment. The wide variety of areas that innovation in sports occurs means it is important to understand the environmental context that influences the innovation. Innovation plays an important role in sport management as it adds enhancements to the field.

One of the major ways sport has become innovative is through information technology, which is used in team management, scheduling and tracking revenue (Barneva and Hite, 2017). Moreover, information technology has enabled the use of websites to encourage more information sharing about athletes, teams and viewers. More recently, there has been interest in data analytics, particularly for event management and performance reports. This is due to data analytics in sport being able to assist decision making through analyzing key trends and projections. Sport has changed from the use of data analytics that help estimate player performance but also the projected profitability of certain players. Table 8.3 depicts the major types of information technology innovations in sport.

Due to the embryonic status of sports innovation, there needs to be more analysis of its processes. Innovation is widely diffused into sport as it is recognized as a driver of competitiveness. Innovation is necessary to the success of sports organizations as it keeps up to date with change. The transfer of innovation into sport is the result of the need for more business applications in the health and wellness industry. Innovation provides sport with the attributes necessary to be successful in the global market. The use of innovation in sport is still underutilized and needs more attention. Innovation can add to the body of knowledge about sport by preparing for future trends.

Innovation systems are important to sport especially in terms of sharing and disseminating knowledge. Hekkert et al (2007:415) state "the central idea behind the IS approach is that innovation and diffusion of technology is both an individual and a collective act." This is relevant in sport innovation as it acknowledges the role of the innovator needing help from other sources. This can include institutions and government bodies that help influence the rate of innovation. These institutions need to diffuse, import, initiate and modify new technologies by providing a network structure between private and public sectors (Freeman, 1987).

The systems view of innovation highlights how it often takes time to develop and needs help from other sources in order for it to lead to commercialization. Innovation often follows a certain path because of the existing use of innovation within a sports context. This means that cost and performance decisions related

TABLE 8.3 Information technology innovations in sport

Type	Functions
Accounting and finance	Payment, forms, registration
Athletic coaching	Player performance, team management
Data analytics	Predicting future performance, training of players
Event management	Preparation for tournaments
Facility management	Coordination of functions
Financial strategies	Revenue and profitability prediction
Personnel management	Analysis of staff
Public relations	Social media marketing
Risk management	Insurance
Team management	Collection of players and reports

Source: Adapted from Barneva and Hite (2017).

to the innovation need to be taken into account. This includes analyzing how the socio-economic environment helps or hinders the progress of sports innovation. Kemp (1994) refers to the socio-economic environment as including capital outlays, skills, knowledge, infrastructure, production routines, lifestyles, social norms and regulations. This means there are many factors in the socio-economic environment that affect the sports innovation system.

Sports innovation development is not an independent process but requires the management of innovation systems. The design of sports innovation management processes is a key issue in the successful implementation of the innovation. Hekkert et al (2007:414) define innovation systems as "a heuristic attempt, developed to analyze all societal subsystems, actors and institutions contributing in one way or the other, directly or indirectly, intentionally or not, to the emergence or production of innovation." This means that, in a sport context, innovation systems are a complex set of interrelationships that need to be managed properly. People watch sport but are also motivated by the feelings derived from the consumption. This means that sports innovation can occur in a linear manner when people watch the sport but also in a dyadic manner when they are involved in fantasy sport or user-driven sport in which they participate in the co-creation process.

The concepts of sport and innovation have their own specific literature and can be studied independently but benefit when they are analyzed together. This is because sport and innovation are closely related as a result of the processes and products involved in both. In both sport and innovation there are explicit streams of research dealing with each of these topics but often there is an underlying link to the other topic area. This means when studying sport or innovation there is an implicit relationship with the other topic area.

Winand and Fergusson (2016:1) state "the world of sport has embraced the new waves of decision-aid technology, designed to help referees and officials make the right decision." These decision-aid technologies are utilized in a range of sports including instant replay and tracking a ball's trajectory. In sport, use of referees' decisions and decision-aid technology are combined because of the performance implications of the right decision being made. However, some sports, notably football, have been slow to adopt decision-aid technology and this has been criticized as it could have helped with making the right decisions.

The introduction of decision-aid technology into sport has met with some debate, particularly around the philosophy of using technology in a human-centered activity. Traditionally umpiring has been conducted based on experience and intuition but the introduction of decision-aid technology has changed sport (Collins, 2010). There has been an increased demand from sport spectators to use decision-aid technology and it has become part of the viewing experience. This is seen in the use of decision-aid technology being part of tennis with spectators expecting its use. In 2010, the International Football Association Board (IFAB) agreed to introduce decision-aid technology into games (Winand and Fergusson, 2016). There are two major decision-aid technologies utilized in football: Hawkeye and GoalRef (Winand and Fergusson, 2016). The Hawkeye goal system enables the tracking of play on a football pitch while GoalRef uses a chip within the ball to track where it goes.

There are different stakeholders concerned with the use of technology innovations in sport. These include spectators who prefer to experience the game without the distraction of technology. Although some technological innovations take time to be accepted, there has been a recent demand by spectators for more technology use in sport. This is the result of some controversial referee decisions that could have been avoided if an impartial decision-aid technology had been used.

The use of technologies such as smartwatches is a new concept in sport. Most sport management research continues to be dominated by a physical education approach rather than an entrepreneurial or innovation perspective. Wearable fitness technology is becoming more popular, especially in the form of watches that can test for physical forms of fitness such as blood pressure in addition to more traditional features such as telling the time.

Implications for practice

The rise of technology in sport has several important implications for practice. Spearing the playing of sport to the integration of technology within it might help people understand the complementary nature of sports with technology innovation. Seeing the effects of technology innovation in sport can help increase understanding about the changing nature of sport management. Sports organizations that want to intentionally integrate technology innovations into sport need to find mechanisms that facilitate the process.

Technology and associated applications relating to sport are fundamental to sports business. However, there is still a lack of understanding about the policies and business development of sports technology innovation. This means there is still a lot to discover about sports technology innovation. This chapter highlights the complex and interesting nature of sports technology innovation. The diversity of research themes relevant to sports technology are explained. Given the allure of technology to sport, it is important to understand how technology innovation impacts on sport. This will make a contribution to the development of sports technology innovation. It is hoped that this chapter will contribute to our knowledge of sports technology innovation and stimulate more interest in this area.

Technology is impacting the way sport is played and how it is communicated. As technology is reshaping our lives, the way sport interacts with technology is changing. This is seen with the increasing popularity of the use of camera technology in sports games. It is anticipated that in the future there will be more technological innovations that will further change the role of sport in society. In order to examine the role of sport business, the influence of technology innovation in sport should be examined. An understanding of technology innovation in sport business is central to our knowledge of the changing nature of sport.

Conclusion

In conclusion, this chapter has drawn on technology innovation theory and practice to link to the sports field. More work is needed on how technology innovations are envisioned and embedded in a sports context. The results offered in this chapter contribute to the development of a body of research about sports technology innovation. An interesting question here is, how can technology innovation be evaluated in sport, which has a high level of non-profit organizations that work together with profit organizations? This question is an interesting issue for technological innovations that will substantially change the way we see and view sport.

This chapter has contributed to the ongoing debate about how to incorporate technological innovation in sport. The utilization of a technology perspective into sports innovation takes into account the entrepreneurial activity occurring in technology. This means that as the technology innovation literature has been somewhat overlooked in previous research, this chapter adds to our understanding of sports innovation management. In addition, this chapter has provided initial insights into how sport research can be revitalized utilizing technology innovation studies.

References

Anggadwita, G., Luterlean, B.S., Ramadani, V. and Ratten, V. (2017) 'Socio-cultural environments and emerging economy entrepreneurship: Women entrepreneurs in Indonesia', *Journal of Entrepreneurship in Emerging Economies*, 9(1): 85–96.

Asheim, B.T. and Coenen, L. (2005) Knowledge bases and regional innovation systems: Comparing Nordic clusters', *Research Policy*, 34(8), 1173–1190.

Barneva, R.P. and Hite, P.D. (2017) 'Information technology in sport management curricula', *Journal of Educational Technology*, 45(3): 326–342.

Barrett, P. and Sexton, M. (2006) 'Innovation in small, project-based construction firms', *British Journal of Management*, 17(4), 331–346.

Brown, R., Gregson, G. and Mason, C. (2016) 'A post-mortem of regional innovation policy failure: Scotland's Intermediate Technology Initiative (ITI)', *Regional Studies*, 50(7): 1260–1272.

Caza, A. (2000) 'Context receptivity: Innovation in an amateur sport organization', *Journal of Sport Management*, 14: 227–242.

Collins, H. (2010) 'The philosophy of umpiring and the introduction of decision-aid technology', *Journal of the Philosophy of Sport*, 37: 135–146.

Cooke, P. (2016) 'Four minutes to four years: The advantage of recombinant over specialized innovation—RIS3 versus "smartspec"', *European Planning Studies*, 24(8): 1494–1510.

D'Antone, S., Canning, L., Franklin-Johnson, E. and Spencer, R. (2017) 'Concerned innovation: The ebb and flow between market and society', *Industrial Marketing Management*, https://doi.org/10.1016/j.indmarman.2017.02.006.

Floyd, S.W. and Lane, P.J. (2000) 'Strategizing throughout the organization: Managing role conflict in strategic renewal', *Academy of Management Review*, 25: 154–177.

Freeman, C. (1987) *Technology Policy and Economic Performance: Lessons from Japan*, Pinter Publishers Ltd, London.

Hekkert, M.P., Suurs, R.A., Negro, S.O., Kuhlmann, S. and Smits, R.E. (2007) 'Functions of innovation systems: A new approach for analyzing technological change', *Technological Forecasting & Social Change*, 74: 413–432.

Huggins, R. and Prokop, D. (2016) 'Network structure and regional innovation: A study of university-industry ties', *Urban Studies*, 1: 1–22.

Jensen, M.B., Johnson, B. and Lorenz, E. (2007) 'Forms of knowledge and modes of innovation', *Research Policy*, 36(5): 680–693.

Johannessen, J-A., Olsen, B. and Lumpkin, G.T. (2001) 'Innovation as newness: What is new, how new and new to whom?', *European Journal of Innovation Management*, 4(1): 20–31.

Kemp, R. (1994) 'Technology and the transition to environmental sustainability—the problem of technological regime shifts', *Futures*, 26(10): 1023–1046.

Kimberly, J.R. and Evanisko, M.J. (1981) 'Organizational innovation: The influence of individual, organizational and contextual factors on hospital adoption of technological and administrative innovations', *Academy of Management Journal*, 24: 689–713.

Lanzolla, G. and Suarez, F.F. (2012) 'Closing the technology adoption use divide: The role of contiguous user bandwagon', *Journal of Management*, 38: 836–859.

McDonald, H., Leckie, C., Karg, A., Zubcevic-Basic, N. and Lock, D. (2016) 'Segmenting initial fans of a new team: A taxonomy of sport early adopters', *Journal of Consumer Behavior*, 15: 136–148.

Morrison, A. (2000) 'Entrepreneurship: What triggers it?', *International Journal of Entrepreneurial Behaviour & Research*, 6(2): 59–71.

Parent, M.M., Rovillard, C. and Naraine, M.L. (2016) 'Network governance of a multi-level, multi-sectoral sport event: Differences in coordinating ties and actors', *Sport Management Review*, https://doi.org/10.1016/j.smr.2017.02.001.

Pettigrew, A., Ferlie, E. and McKee, L. (1992) *Shaping Strategic Change*, SAGE, London.

Quinn, J.B. (1985) 'Managing innovations controlled chaos', *Harvard Business Review*, May–June: 73–84.

Rogers, E.M. (2003) *Diffusion of Innovation*, 5th ed, Free Press, New York.

Rule, E.G. and Irwin, D.W. (1988) 'Fostering intrapreneurship: The new competitive ease', *Journal of Business Strategy*, 9(3): 14–47.

Seifried, C., Katz, M. and Tutka, P. (2016) 'A conceptual model on the process of innovation diffusion through a historical review of the United States Armed Forces and their bowl game', *Sport Management Review*, https://doi.org/10.1016/j.smr.2016.10.009

Sexton, M. and Barrett, P. (2003) 'A literature synthesis of innovation in small construction firms: Insights, ambiguities and questions', *Construction Management and Economics*, 21(6), 613–622.

Tajeddini, K. and Ratten, V. (2017) 'The moderating effect of brand orientation on inter-firm market orientation and performance', *Journal of Strategic Marketing*, 1–31.

Tsiotsou, R. and Ratten, V. (2010) 'Future research directions in tourism marketing', *Marketing Intelligence & Planning*, 28(4): 533–544.

Winand, M. and Fergusson, C. (2016) 'More decision-aid technology in sport? An analysis of football supporters perceptions on goal-line technology', *Soccer & Society*, 1–20.

9
FUTURE DIRECTIONS FOR SPORTS INNOVATION MANAGEMENT

Introduction

This book represents a collective effort to understand the nature and meaning of innovation in sport. In the last chapter of this book, I focus on the range of activities that constitute sports innovation management. This approach serves to highlight areas that need more attention in terms of connecting the sports and innovation management literature. This will help build a theory of sports innovation that can encourage more practical and academic interest in sports innovation management.

Different innovation perspectives were drawn together in this book in a coherent way to examine sports innovation. Sports innovation is a diverse topic that has different meanings according to the context. This complexity of sports innovation means that it is important to understand what type of innovation is being utilized in the sport context. Sports innovation is dynamic and brings new energy into the sports and innovation disciplines. There are important reasons for sport to utilize an innovation paradigm as a result of its role in social and economic development.

Sports innovation seeks to engage sport as an innovator in order to introduce new ideas. This book has focused on sports innovation because it provides a way to combine sport and innovation that integrates unique characteristics. Innovation does influence the nature of sport because of its ability to create change that leads to performance improvements. In this book, I have examined sports innovation by providing examples of different dimensions exhibiting diversity. Innovation in sport can represent different forms from which the sports innovation is manifested, including product, process, social, organizational and environmental.

It is essential to identify new avenues about sports innovation to be explored in future research. While considerable progress has been made on innovation management, there are manifestations inherent in sport that are yet to be explored, which provides the reason for this book. Innovation is the buzzword in the media and is especially important to sport (Ratten, 2017a). Despite the popularity of sports innovation there has been little research about its meaning and application in both a theoretical and practical sense. This chapter fills the gap in the literature linking future possibilities for innovation in a sports context. The suggestions are for sport and innovation to connect more in a way that develops the sports innovation field. This will help anyone interested in sport to develop a more innovative mindset.

Contributions of this book

The contributions of this book are in three distinct areas. First, the contents of the book demonstrate the various types of innovation that affect sport. Innovation in sport has evolved based on the technological and social developments that have affected the industry. This book helps extend the role of innovation to a sport context by considering evolutionary perspectives on innovation and the role of cooperation. Second, the book integrates the innovation literature into the sport context to create a new discipline of sports innovation. Rather than considering sport and innovation two different disciplines, the book considers the interrelationships between both as a mechanism to help improve the understanding about sports innovation.

An integrative approach combining the sports and innovation literature with an emphasis on their complementary nature was used. This allowed the development of sports innovation to be continually discussed in the book. The synthesized nature of innovation in sport was analyzed as a way of moving forward the field of sports innovation. Finally, the future of sports innovation as a topic of dissemination was presented that tied together the disparate sport and innovation areas of business. This included practical suggestions about how sport organizations can become more innovative over time. This extends innovation into the sport context by demonstrating that sport is inherently innovative and needs to respond to change in a creative way.

Sports and innovation management

Sport management is dynamic and complex due to the diversity of sports-related activities. Sport requires an innovative approach to its management style as it has developed from being a purely recreational activity to being a business. This has led to sport managers being more focused on underlying business decisions that involve innovative developments. As a result of the increased interest of sports managers on profit maximization this has involved more interest in the process of innovation as to how it can influence further commercialization and differentiation of sport business.

The ultimate aim of sports innovation research is to develop a theory that can be used in future studies. The theory of sports innovation should incorporate a creativity perspective due to the different types of change that exist in sport. The emphasis on innovation in the global economy is valuable to sport as it provides a rationale for changing behavior. Sports management can be described by innovation theory due to the commitment toward increasing performance. According to sports innovation theory, managers desire creative solutions to problems that address future possible revenue areas. The intensity of the sports innovation will depend on the contextual factors and situational characteristics.

The differences in innovation between non-sports and sports organizations need to be more properly understood. This will help in designing innovation policies that are better implemented in the sports context. This book has advocated sports innovation studies that detail the creativity activities within sport.

TABLE 9.1 Future directions of sport innovation research

Theme	Ideas
Commercialization	What ways is sport becoming more business-orientated?
	How to expand ideas from non-profit sport entities into commercial ventures?
	What is the interplay between social, non-profit and commercial sport?
Consumer experience	How do consumers co-create sports innovation?
	What types of sports innovations are consumers helping to develop?
Demographic changes	What is the role of urban and rural living in sports innovation?
	How are different age groups adapting to sport innovation?
Health issues	How are health-related issues becoming important in sport (e.g., fitness tracking)?
	What technological sport innovations are being developed for health reasons?
Individualization	How are individuals innovating sport due to their personal preferences?
	What is the role of individual characteristics in sports innovation?
Internationalization	How has international cultural differences impacted sports innovation?
	What is the role of media in disseminating sports innovation?
Social	How are sports innovations helping people in developing countries?
	What is the role of the non-profit sector in sports innovation?
Technology	What new and emerging technologies are affecting sports innovation?
	What is the role of the Internet of Things in sport innovation?

This approach can involve a comparison of innovation activities with non-sport entities. By identifying the innovation differences in innovation processes it will help to understand the decisions sports organizations make toward change. As innovation requires action it will help to verify the role of sports in facilitating innovative behavior. Table 9.1 states some suggested future directions for sport innovation research.

The ability to achieve some level of innovation in sports organizations is necessary to achieve efficiency. This helps to create new knowledge and ensure successful performance in sport. The concepts of sport and innovation are imbued with added complexity as a result of changing market conditions. Moreover, sports innovation is reliant on the dynamic interaction between sport and innovation in a changing global business environment that is increasingly reliant on technology.

The desire to progress competitively is at the heart of many sports organizations. This means that sports innovation can generate long-term change and a difference in the way decisions are made within organizations. Sport organizations have unique resources that affect the way innovation is utilized. As innovation can vary depending on the context, it helps to understand the objectives of sports organizations (Ratten, 2017b). The distinct characteristics of sports organizations mean that there may be an urgent need to explore innovation.

Suggestions for future research

Based on the chapters of this book, there are ample areas of future research focusing on sports innovation. There is a lot of scope to exploit more connection between sport and innovation. These suggestions are outlined below. To begin with, there needs to be a more deliberate focus on innovation as the theoretical foundation for sport studies about sport. This provides attention placed on the competences associated with innovation in the sports context. As discussed in previous chapters of this book, innovation is required in sport to build performance. The innovation can be refined to account for different sports contexts that might be more inclined to explore innovation.

There needs to be more linkage between the practice of sport and innovation ecosystems. An understanding of the different organizational structures in sport that help or hinder innovation is needed. An interesting area to study are the innovation processes that have enabled some sports organizations to flourish. This could put pressure on sports organizations to recognize the benefit of an innovation culture. While there is a considerable amount of literature on innovation management, more consideration of the unique aspect of sport is required. In sport, there is often a leader that affects the flow of the organization or teams. This means that an understanding of leadership can sharpen our knowledge of how it relates to sports innovation. For example, is it athletes themselves or the team managers that are the instigators of innovation? Or does innovation in sport require a combination of athletes and marketing personnel to ensure its success?

Overall, sports innovation research would benefit from incorporating more process and context-driven studies about how innovation is different in a sports context. While there has been some work on sports innovation, there is a lack of consensus about it as a theoretical framework for future research. This book will help to build sports innovation as a theoretical framework to connect the disparate sports and innovation literatures. More effort could be made to extrapolate the associations between sport and innovation, particularly in the global business context. An innovation focus on sports can uncover the capabilities of sports organizations to be innovative.

This book on sports innovation management has revealed the opportunities to bridge the sport and innovation fields of study and practice. Research on sports innovation has the potential to change the direction of the field of sports management. This will enrich conversations about the practical role of innovation in sport. There are a number of future research areas that will provide interesting avenues. This will help build useful understandings about the relevance of innovation to sport.

Summary

In this chapter, there were three important trends discussed relevant to the development of sports innovation management. First, the approach to understanding and defining sports innovation was stated. This helped to focus on the distinct nature of sports innovation compared to other types of innovation. There is a value to defining sports innovation as a key way to understand the complex and dynamic nature of the sports industry. More research and practical emphasis will be placed on sports innovation in the future as it is the essence of competitiveness that is integral to sport.

Second, the literature about whether innovation affects sports performance was reviewed. This included an examination of the different types of innovation in sport and whether this influences performance. Innovation occurs in a variety of different ways in sport and organizations need to be mindful of how to develop their innovative capability.

Third, a theory of sports innovation in a management context was stated. Based on the examples of sports innovation in different contexts there are distinct advantages for focusing on innovation in sport. Sport is a complex field and differs at the individual, regional and international level. This means that it is encouraging to see sports innovation develop as a distinct discipline applying both the sport and innovation fields of study. As discussed in this book, sports innovation theory relies on the assumption that change is necessary for organizational survival. Therefore, there is potential to integrate an innovation perspective more closely into sport to obtain a better understanding of the conditions affecting innovation. This can help direct more attention to the untapped ways to use innovation in sport.

Conclusion

This chapter has summarized the future directions of sport innovation, which is important given the emerging technological developments affecting sport. The chapters in this book are organized into topics related to the process of sports innovation. Each chapter enables a more holistic theory of sports innovation to develop. Thus, the chapters in this book represent a conceptual and practical understanding of sports innovation. There appear to be many interesting factors that will further fuel the growth of sports innovation. The role of innovators, organizations, athletes, teams and governments in promoting innovation in sport were discussed. I hope this book continues to spur more interest in sports innovation as an important topic in the global knowledge economy.

References

Ratten, V. (2017a) *Entrepreneurship and Innovation in Smart Cities*, Routledge, London.

Ratten, V. (2017b) 'Social media innovations and creativity', in Brem, A. and Viardot, E. (Eds) *Revolution of Innovation Management*, pp. 199–220, Palgrave, London.

INDEX

absorptive capacity 24
acceptance finding (in creative process) 20
adhocracy culture 35
adoption process of innovation 8
ambitious entrepreneurs 53

brand innovation 51
business, sport as 82–3
business model innovation 41–2
business model reconstruction 90
business performance of sport industry 6
buzz marketing 50

change, innovation and 38, 46
clan culture 35
closed innovation 74
co-creation 23–4
cognitive factors in innovation 30
collective learning 39–40
confirmation stage (decision process) 104
connections within sport industry 6
consumer health-fitness sport services 32
consumer innovativeness 46
consumer pleasure sport services 32
contexts of innovation 8–10
coordination capability 24
corporate entrepreneurship in sport 86–90; defined 88; implications for sports managers 94; innovation milieus 92–4; lack of literature on 80–1; organizational culture and 88–9; portfolio entrepreneurship 92; stages of **91**; strategic entrepreneurship 90–1; types of 87
creative process, steps in 20

creativity: defined 38; innovation and entrepreneurship versus 21
creativity in sport 15–17, 19–21, **21**; co-creation 23–4; proactive personalities 22–3
crystallization of culture 71
cultural context for sport 8, 59–60
culture: of organizations 35–7, 71, 88–9; of sports innovation 107–8, 111–13, **112**
customer experiences 64–5

decision process for sports innovation 103–4
decision-aid technology 115
diffusion of innovation 102
disruptive innovation 61
dissemination of creativity 21
distributed innovation systems 74–5
domain redefinition 90

ecology of sports innovation 60–1
entertainment in sport 4
entrepreneurial ecosystems 35–7
entrepreneurial imitation 87
entrepreneurial intentions 92
entrepreneurial marketing 49–50
entrepreneurial reproduction 86
entrepreneurship: ambitious entrepreneurs 53; creativity and innovation versus 21; defined 86; innovation and 83; intrapreneurship 100–2; sport and 83; sports knowledge in 26–7; types of 86–7; *see also* corporate entrepreneurship in sport

environmental factors in innovation 30
e-service innovation 33
explicit knowledge 25–6, 105
exploitation 25–6
exploration 25

fact finding (in creative process) 20
failure in innovation process 89
future: research suggestions 120–3, **121**; of sports management 13

guerrilla marketing 49–50

hierarchical culture 35
human curative services 33
human excellence services 32
human skills services 32
human sustenance services 32

idea finding (in creative process) 20
idealized influence 34
implementation stage (decision process) 104
inclusive innovation 104
incremental innovations 17
individualized consideration 34
individual-oriented perspective 37
information technology innovation in sport 113–14, **114**
innovation: approaches to 37–8; change and 38, 46; creativity and entrepreneurship versus 21; defined 7; entrepreneurship and 83; newness and 46; phases of 7; success and 46
innovation in sport: adoption process 8; barriers to 41; benefits of 11–12; business performance of 6; co-creation 23–4; contexts of 8–10; contributions of book to 120; creative process 20; culture and 59–60, 107–8; diffusion of 102; disruptive innovation 61; distributed innovation systems 74–5; ecology of 60–1; elements of 46, 70–1; environmental factors 30; explained 53–6; features of sport industry 5; as future of sports management 13; future research suggestions 120–3, **121**; incremental innovations 17; in international markets 30; knowledge sharing 24–6; lack of literature on 26–7; managing 61–4, **64**; marketing in sport context 51–3; need for 45; open innovation 69, 71–4; personality traits for **23**; problems in 77–8; process innovation in 47; product originality in 47; product usefulness in 46–7; relationship between sport and innovation 84–6; social capital and 65–6; social issues and 111–13; societal aspect of 58–9, 76–7; stages of 62; strategic orientation of 44; sustainability 66–7; in team environment 31; technological innovation 47–9, 76; types of 3–5, 17–19; user experiences 64–5; user innovations 10–11; *see also* corporate entrepreneurship in sport; leadership in sports innovation; marketing innovation; technology innovation in sport
innovation milieus 92–4
innovativeness 46
inspirational motivation 34
institutional context for sport 8–9
institutional innovation 19
intellectual stimulation 34
intensity of culture 71
interactions in sports innovation 38–9
interactive perspective 37–8
international markets, innovation in sport in 30
intrapreneurship 100–2
invention, innovation versus 7

Kelly Slater Foundation 111
knowledge sharing 24–6, 38–9, 105
knowledge stage (decision process) 103

leadership in sports innovation: business model innovation 41–2; interactions in 38–9; lack of literature on 31–2; organizational culture 35–7, **36**; sport services 32–3; sport start-ups 39–40; transformational leadership 33–5
live streaming 49

managing sports innovation 61–4, **64**
market culture 35
marketing innovation 18, 44–5; brand innovation 51; entrepreneurial marketing 49–50; in sport context 51–3
measurement areas of innovation management **64**

newness, innovation and 46
non-receptive context 101

open innovation 69, 71–4
organizational culture 35–7, **36**, 71, 88–9
organizational innovation 18
organizational process innovation 47
organizational rejuvenation 90

participant services 32
personal factors in innovation 30
personality traits for sports innovation **23**
persuasion stage (decision process) 103
physical environment, corporate entrepreneurship in sport and 93
policy innovation 19
portfolio entrepreneurship 92
proactive personalities 22–3
problem finding (in creative process) 20
problems in innovation 77–8
process change 33
process innovation 17–18, 47
product innovation 17, 46–7
product originality 47
product usefulness 46–7
promotion of creativity 19

Quiksilver partnership (Kelly Slater case study) 110

receptive context 101
regional innovation systems 105–7
relational capability 24
relationship learning 26
relationships in sports innovation 38–9, 70

service customization 33
sharing knowledge *see* knowledge sharing
Slater, Kelly (surfing case study) 108–11
social capital 65–6
social context of sport 9
social factors in innovation 30, 76–7
social innovation 66
social issues, sport and 111–13
solution finding (in creative process) 20
spatial context of sport 9–10
spectator services 33, 77
sport: benefits of innovation 11–12; as business 82–3; business performance of 6; connections within 6; creativity in 15–17, 19–21, **21**; defined 4; entrepreneurship and 83; features of 5;
relationship with innovation 84–6; social issues and 111–13; types of innovation in 3–5, 17–19; *see also* innovation in sport
sport services 32–3
sport start-ups 39–40; attributes of **40**
sports knowledge in entrepreneurship 26–7
sports management: future of 13; future research suggestions 120–3, **121**; implications of corporate entrepreneurship 94; relationship between sport and innovation 84–6; technology innovation and 113–16
strategic entrepreneurship 90–1
strategic renewal 90
structural perspective 37
success, innovation and 46
surfing case study (Kelly Slater) 108–11
sustainability 47, 66–7
sustained rejuvenation 90
systems of innovation perspective 38

tacit knowledge 25–6, 105
team environment in innovation 31, 88
technology: defined 48; distributed innovation systems 74–5; in process innovation 47; in sports creativity 19, 20
technology innovation in sport 47–9, 76; action and reaction in **98**; culture of 107–8; decision process 103–4; implications for practice 116; inclusive innovation 104; intrapreneurship 100–2; Kelly Slater case study 108–11; knowledge sharing 105; lack of literature on 99–100; process of 98; regional innovation systems 105–7; sports management and 113–16
transformational leadership 33–5

user experiences 64–5
user innovations 10–11

viral marketing 50